GARDENING BY MONTH

A Monthly Guide to Planning the Northeastern & Mid-Atlantic Garden

Copyright © 2021 by Lee Miller

All rights reserved. No part of this publication may be reproduced, distributed, or transmitted in any form or by any means, including photocopying, recording, or other electronic or mechanical methods, without the prior written permission of the author, except in the case of brief quotations embodied in critical reviews and certain other noncommercial uses permitted by copyright law. All images included are © Lee Miller, except where individual credit is given.

Publisher: CreateSpace Independent Publishing

ISBN: 9798571802697

Printed in the United States of America

GARDENING BY MONTH

A Monthly Guide to Planning the Northeastern &
Mid-Atlantic Garden

Lee Miller

GARDENING BY MONTH

This book is dedicated to my husband Tony, who has always stood by my side and encouraged me in everything I do. He has been my rock and best friend all these years and has not only been patient with me while writing each one of my books but has given me the strength and encouragement I need along the way. Thank you for being there!

GARDENING BY MONTH

~About the Author~

Lee Miller is a landscape/garden designer, consultant, and garden blog author from the south shore of Long Island who has been involved in the horticultural industry for over twenty-five years. Her award-winning gardening blog features over 300 articles on general gardening, landscape design principles, gardening tips, planting, pruning, garden maintenance, feature plants and more. Lee is the author of *A Guide to Northeastern Gardening*, *Landscape Design Combinations* and *Dream, Garden, Grow*, each sharing her experiences and know-how as a seasoned gardener. She is now proud to share *Gardening by Month: A Monthly Guide to Planning the Northeastern & Mid-Atlantic Garden*.

GARDENING BY MONTH

GARDENING BY MONTH

Table of Contents

How to Use This Book 9

Chapter 1: Introduction-The Northeastern and Mid-Atlantic Planting Regions 11

Chapter 2: The January-February Garden 19

Chapter 3: The March Garden: Welcome Spring! 27

Chapter 4: The April Garden 39

Chapter 5: The May Garden 51

Chapter 6: The June Garden: Summer Blooms 71

Chapter 7: The July Garden 97

Chapter 8: The August Garden 119

Chapter 9: The September Garden: Fall Interest 131

Chapter 10: The October Garden 141

Chapter 11: The November-December Garden: Winter Has Arrived 155

Chapter 12: Plant Maintenance Tips 175

Index: 182

GARDENING BY MONTH

GARDENING BY MONTH

How to Use This Book

Gardening by Month is a reference for gardeners in the Northeastern and Mid-Atlantic planting regions, organizing horticultural interest by month. This helpful guide is divided into three main sections. First is an introduction to soil types and hardiness zones specific to the Northeast and mid-Atlantic states. Such topics including soil identification, productivity, improvement and maintenance will be discussed.

Next, is an accumulation of over 120 successfully tested plants organized by monthly interest with detailed descriptions of each. Color photographs are accompanied by information on hardiness zone, lighting and watering needs, bloom time and maintenance, along with other noteworthy features.

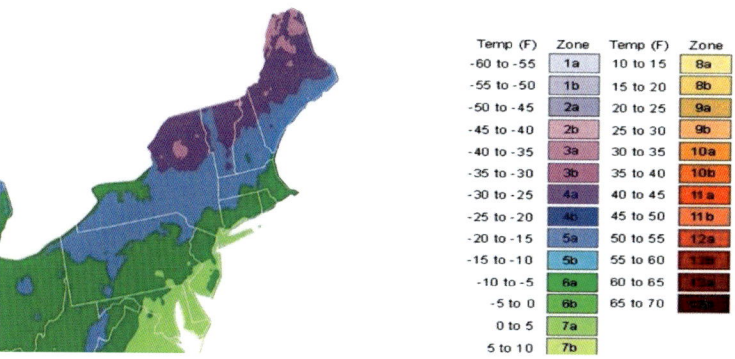

Accompanying plant photographs and descriptions are symbols implemented to organize and facilitate your browsing

GARDENING BY MONTH

experience. This comprehensive reference includes a quick view of lighting requirements, watering needs and additional information including drought tolerance, deer resistance, and bird, butterfly/hummingbird friendliness. When it comes to deer resistance, please note that results may vary by overall deer population and amount of available food, especially when resources are scarce in early spring. In some cases, I have found that plants listed as deer resistant, may be initially browsed upon when it comes to new foliage or blooms. I will happily share my knowledge and experiences with you within each plant description. Additionally, I will share experiences on monthly garden maintenance and specific care for the health of individual plants.

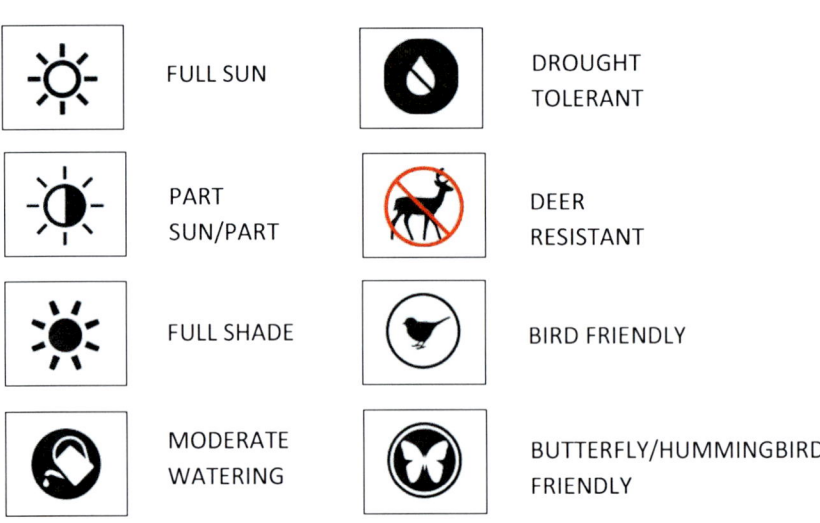

Lastly, this book covers plant and lawn maintenance, with answers to frequently asked questions on disease and insect control, pruning, watering, fertilization, and winter care.

GARDENING BY MONTH

Chapter 1: Introduction-The Northeastern and Mid-Atlantic Planting Regions

As a lifetime gardener and landscape designer for over 25 years, my goal is to create landscapes that provide interest throughout every month of the year. While there are many plant references, I wanted to create a monthly guide that would provide a listing of trees, shrubs and perennials that provide flowers, berries, or some other interest throughout the northeastern and mid-Atlantic growing regions of the United States. The plants being highlighted are hardy in a range of zones from USDA hardiness zones 3-9 and are grouped according to initial bloom time or time of peak interest when it comes to foliage and or fruiting. The information presented can be applied to areas extending beyond the northeast and mid-Atlantic, but keep in mind that initial bloom time or time of interest may vary slightly due to environmental conditions and zone.

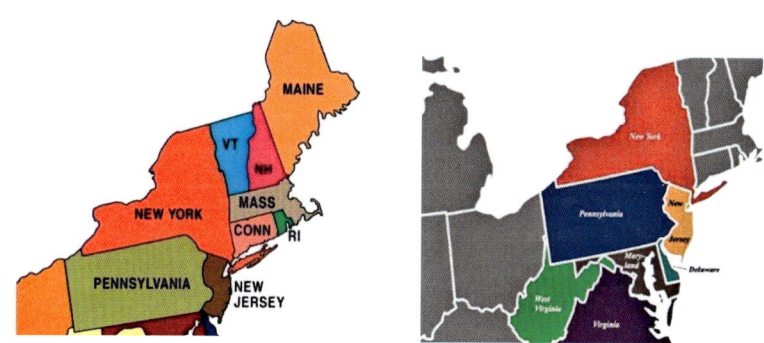

FIGURE 1

For point of reference, the Northeastern planting region (Figure 1 left) includes areas in northern New York, New Jersey, Maine, Vermont, New Hampshire, Massachusetts, Connecticut, Rhode Island, and northern Pennsylvania. The

GARDENING BY MONTH

Mid-Atlantic planting region (Figure 1 right) includes southern New York, Pennsylvania, New Jersey, Maryland, Delaware, Virginia, and West Virginia. There is some overlapping between areas due to microclimates caused by fluctuations in elevation and closeness to a body of water within each state.

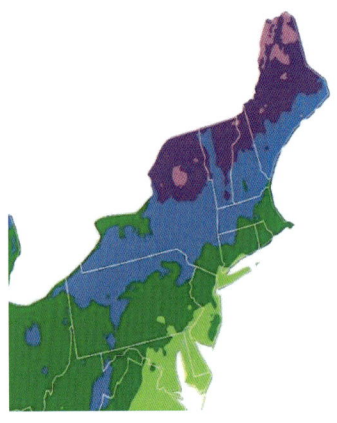

FIGURE 2

HARDINESS ZONES: The Northeastern and Mid-Atlantic states cover a diverse range of microclimates and hardiness zones ranging from USDA zones 3b to 7b. Conditions vary from the most northern regions of Maine, New Hampshire and Vermont (USDA zones 3a-5a) experiencing extremes from warm, humid summers to harsh winters with a possible 60 to 120 inches of snowfall in the higher elevations, to the more southern regions which have fewer temperature extremes and are mostly USDA hardiness zones 5a-7b. When planning your garden, always be sure to check your plant hardiness zone from the U.S. Department of Agriculture (Figure 2 top and bottom) while taking microclimates into consideration. More northern or more southern areas may experience a possible 2 to 4 week difference in initial bloom

Temp (F)	Zone	Temp (F)	Zone
-60 to -55	1a	10 to 15	8a
-55 to -50	1b	15 to 20	8b
-50 to -45	2a	20 to 25	9a
-45 to -40	2b	25 to 30	9b
-40 to -35	3a	30 to 35	10a
-35 to -30	3b	35 to 40	10b
-30 to -25	4a	40 to 45	11a
-25 to -20	4b	45 to 50	11b
-20 to -15	5a	50 to 55	12a
-15 to -10	5b	55 to 60	12b
-10 to -5	6a	60 to 65	13a
-5 to 0	6b	65 to 70	13b
0 to 5	7a		
5 to 10	7b		

time, but the ordering of blooms will remain the same. Also keep in mind that the plants you purchase should have a cold or heat hardiness that falls somewhere in between those indicated for your zone. For example, if you are in zone 7a, try to purchase plants that will tolerate colder temperatures down to zones 4 or 5 and warmer temperatures up to zone 8. Purchasing a plant that is hardy to zone 7 will mean that it is borderline should a colder winter occur.

SOIL TYPES: A good soil consists of various components combined in the correct proportions. Most garden plantings prefer a loam soil with a balance of various sized particles, ideally 40% sand, 40% silt and 20% clay, with adequate organic matter and pore space. Most of the soil in the northeastern and mid-Atlantic planting regions has been deposited by glacial activity and consists of a mixture of clay, clay mixtures, silt, sand, gravel (from granular size to larger) and boulders in different proportions. The first, clay is the smallest particle size with a diameter of less than .002mm. It is often orangey in color and sticks easily to your hands. If you have a moist soil sample and can roll it in your hand to form a two to three-inch-long ribbon, then there is a good chance of significant clay content. This is important to note because clay particles are smaller, closer together and with smaller pore spaces between them, making drainage more difficult. A dominantly clay soil is rich in nutrients but will tend to hold moisture for a longer time. This can affect the amount of oxygen taken up by plant roots. Next, silt is a medium sized particle (0.002-0.05mm) and feels comparable to the texture of dry flour. Lastly, sand is the largest and coarsest of the soil particle sizes (ranging from .05 to 2.00 mm) with the largest spacing between particles, resulting is less moisture storage capacity and rapid drainage.

GARDENING BY MONTH

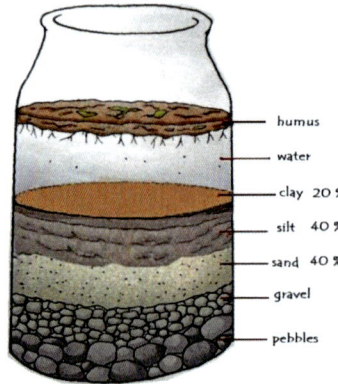

FIGURE 3

An easy way to determine soil type is to obtain a glass container (Figure 3) and fill it approximately two-thirds full of water. Add enough soil to nearly fill the jar and shake vigorously. Then, allow the container to sit for a couple of days until you see layers forming. (Note: There may be some clay floating at the top.) Measure the height of each layer and the overall height of the soil and divide the first by the later to get a percentage. Use the USDA Soil Triangle (Figure 4) to determine your soil type. Draw lines for each percentage of soil type in your sample, and where the three lines converge is your soil composition.

IMPROVING SOIL CONDITIONS: Adding organic material can help to remedy a variety of soil problems. When planting, backfill with an organic enriched topsoil containing

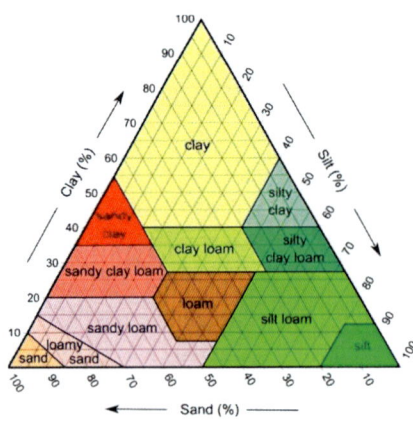

FIGURE 4

the ideal combination of soil components and organic matter (humus) to give your plantings a good start. Since much of the soil on the north shore of Long Island is sandy and rocky, digging a slightly larger hole around each planting and adding the proper topsoil can help to remedy any problems. If the soil is too compacted with a heavy percentage of clay and there are drainage issues, a sand wick can be dug. To form a sand wick, dig down approximately three feet (at the width of a post hole digger) and fill the hole with sand or gravel. (Note: I have found gravel to work best for problem areas.) The larger sized particles allow for greater pore space and proper drainage, allowing excess water to move away from the roots, where it can sit and cause harm. Sand wicks can be constructed along a planting area or in a lawn to prevent drainage issues and allow sufficient oxygen exchange. For extremely sandy or clay-like soils, the addition of organic matter such as compost can be beneficial by increasing pore space (in clay soil) or decreasing pore space (in sandy soil) while improving drainage.

SOIL pH: Soil pH can be affected by several factors including mineral content, soil texture and climate. Temperature and rainfall affect the pH of soil. Generally, warm humid climates tend to have soils with a lower pH due to abundant rainfall and leaching, while drier climates tend to have more neutral or alkaline soils. Knowing your soil's pH is important because it affects the ability of plants to absorb nutrients and maintain overall health. Most plants require a pH between 6.0 and 7.0; however, some plants such as azalea, rhododendron, conifers, strawberries and blueberries prefer a slightly higher acidic soil (pH 5.0-5.5). For these acid loving plants, a condition known as chlorosis can occur when grown in a soil that is too alkaline. Symptoms include smaller than usual leaves that are pale green or yellow. These signs are similar in appearance to those from nitrogen deficiency, only with pH symptoms, there are still prominent green veins in the leaves. Generally, most ornamental landscape plants grow best in a more neutral to slightly acidic soil (pH 5.8 to 6.5). Some plants such as ferns and asparagus thrive best in a neutral to slightly alkaline soil (pH 6.6-7.5). When purchasing your plants, check the label, which usually indicates pH requirements, and if needed, have your soil tested by a local cooperative extension or use a home soil testing device.

Once you test your soil, there are applications you can easily implement to adjust the acidity or alkalinity. To increase alkalinity, add lime. There are two main types of lime, pelletized and agricultural. Agricultural lime is a coarse limestone best used for large agricultural applications, such as farming and requires an industrial spreader. Pelletized lime is a finer particle lime that can be easily applied with most home lawn spreaders. There is also powdered lime, but this form tends to create a lot of dust and can easily move to places where it is unwanted. To increase acidity, add Aluminum sulfate. Aluminum sulfate is fast acting and will change the pH of your soil immediately as it produces hydrogen ions as soon as it is dissolved in water. Adding organic mulch or peat moss can naturally lower and maintain the acidic condition of your soil.

Overall, the northeastern and Mid-Atlantic planting regions are known to have some of the finest growing conditions in the U.S. due to their reliable soil, relatively moderate winters, and sufficient rainfall, just the ingredients you need to create a successful garden!

GARDENING BY MONTH

GARDENING BY MONTH

GARDENING BY MONTH

Chapter 2: The January-February Garden

The gardening journey begins in January as the beauty of nature's innermost artwork is now more prevalent over other times when foliage is abundant. During the winter months, the twisting structure of trees with their interesting shapes and silhouettes brings on a whole new interest. The texture of exfoliating bark on Crape Myrtle, brilliant red stems of dogwood or the golden-red berries of holly and winterberry continue to shine as new life starts to emerge in the garden. Beneath the leathery evergreen foliage of Hellebores are deep pink buds just waiting to open, while pure white snowdrops continue to show from breaks in the snow, and the season is underway.

From a design standpoint, winter is a time when the "bones" or structure of the garden are most evident. January and February are a time for reflection of the season past and evaluating what is working in the garden and what could use some adjustments during the following season. Look for areas where the garden could use some additional seasonal interest and examine the lighting and moisture for that space before selecting plants.

The winter season is also a time for revitalizing tools, starting seeds, and forcing spring bulbs inside. Clean, sharpen and oil moving parts on gardening tools before you put them away to keep them at their best. Purchase your seeds and sow them in flats or containers indoors by a window, under grow lights, in a greenhouse, or outdoors in a cold frame. Flowers including Petunias, Impatiens and Begonias can be started in January-early February, while edibles including lettuce, kale, chives, tomatoes, and peppers should be sown four to six weeks before the last frost date, which depends on your zone.

GARDENING BY MONTH

AVERAGE FIRST AND LAST FROST DATES:

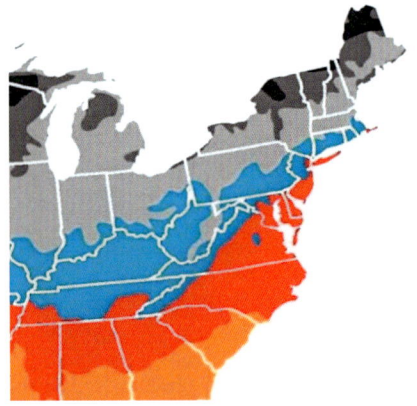

ZONE	3	4	5	6	7	8
AVERAGE FIRST FROST	Sept.1-Sept.30	Sept.1-Sept.30	Sept.30-Oct.30	Sept.30-Oct.30	Sept.30-Oct.30	Oct.30-Nov.30
AVERAGE LAST FROST	May 1-May 31	May 1-May 31	March 30-April 30	March 30-April 30	March 30-April 30	Feb.22-March 30

Spring bulbs can be forced by planting them in a light, well-drained potting mix. Water and allow them to chill in a cool, but not freezing dark spot, such as a cold basement or unheated garage. To chill cold hardy bulbs, they should be stored at 40-60 degrees Fahrenheit for the first three to four weeks after potting, while allowing them chill to between 32-40 degrees afterwards to mimic a drop in soil temperature. Once you see fleshy white roots appearing through the drainage holes, bring them into a lighted room to bloom. Favorite bulbs for forcing include Daffodils, Hyacinths, Tulips and Dwarf Irises.

Outdoors, continue to monitor the garden, keep on top of weeds on those milder days and plan away for the upcoming season!

GARDENING BY MONTH

~JANUARY-FEBRUARY~

HELLEBORUS 'SHOOTING STAR' (LENTEN ROSE)

There can be blooms in winter! Hellebores, also known as Lenten Rose or Christmas Rose, are grown for their interest in the garden while other perennials are dormant. The plants are frost resistant and produce showy blooms starting in January and February. Hellebore 'Shooting Star', hardy in USDA zones 4-9, produces lush evergreen growth with small creamy white flowers with pink highlights. As the flowers age, pink and green coloration develops in the face of the flower. Blooms last a long period of time, lasting through April with multiple waves of flowers. Plants grow to a height and width of 8-12 inches and prefer partial shade. This variety starts blooming early around January-February in the northeast and Mid-Atlantic states. To maintain an attractive plant, remove any winter damaged foliage in springtime. Hellebores are known to be deer resistant.

GALANTHUS (SNOWDROPS)

Galanthus, otherwise known as Snowdrops, are hardy herbaceous perennials that spread by underground bulbs. Snowdrops are one of the first blooms of the season, displaying delicate white upside-down petals that resemble falling snow. These tiny three to six-inch tall plants emerge and bloom just as winter slowly transforms into spring. As each flower opens, three smaller petals open over three inner petals in a white drooping bloom. Symbolizing hope, Galanthus have also been looked upon as an expression of sympathy, purity, optimism, and virtue. The best time to plant Galanthus (Snowdrops) is in autumn, October to November, in a location

GARDENING BY MONTH

with sun to moderate shade and a rich, but well-drained soil. Galanthus is hardy in USDA zones 3-7 and is deer resistant.

IRIS RETICULATA (PHOTO CREDIT WIKIMEDIA COMMONS, AUTHOR MAGNUS MANSKE MAY 2009)

Iris reticulata, also known as reticulated iris or netted iris, is one of the earliest flowers to appear, blooming at the same time as Snowdrops and Snow Crocuses. In late winter to early spring, vibrant petite purplish-blue flowers with yellow centers are displayed above four to six-inch tall grassy foliage on this dwarf cultivar. Plant bulbs in late summer to early fall so that roots can develop before freezing temperatures arrive. Iris reticulata is hardy in USDA zones 5-9 and prefers to be planted in a location with full to partial sun and a well-drained soil. Iris reticulata is perfect for naturalizing and rock gardens, is drought tolerant once established and considered undesirable to deer and rabbits.

HELLEBORUS 'HGC MERLIN' (LENTEN ROSE)

Another later blooming variety of Helleborus, Helleborus 'Merlin' is a sturdy hybrid bred in Germany by Josef Heuger. Hardy in USDA zones 5-9, evergreen foliage lasts throughout the year on 10-12 inch-high by wide plants. Medium pink blooms come about in late February and last throughout April, maturing to a deep cranberry. Like all hellebores, plant in partial shade in a moderately moist soil. Hellebores are known to be deer and rabbit resistant. An interesting fact about Hellebores is that their petals are really sepals, which accounts for the longevity of the blooms.

GARDENING BY MONTH

HAMAMELIS (WITCH HAZEL) PHOTO CREDIT: WIKIMEDIA, AUTHOR SI GRIFFITHS JANUARY 2013

Hardy in USDA zones 5-8, Witch hazels are a genus of flowering plants in the family Hamamelidaceae, with four species in North America, and one each in Japan and China. Witch Hazel is a slow grower, reaching an eventual mature height and width of 10 to 15 feet, while producing fragrant orange-yellow flowers in deep winter. It is known that the best floral colors come from hybrid Hamamelis x intermedia, while Chinese witch hazel (H. mollis) offers the best scent. H. virginiana is known to grow in woodland clearings and is fragrant but not as showy. Grow Hamamelis in a location with full sun and a well-drained soil for best results. To maintain appearance, prune when flowers are spent, before summer.

GARDENING BY MONTH

GARDENING BY MONTH

Chapter 3: The March Garden: Welcome Spring!

Whether March comes in like a lion or a lamb, the garden is getting ready to come out of its winter's sleep. To get your garden prepared for spring, remove any leftover debris and prune back perennials left from last year. Inspect trees and shrubs for damaged branches. Prune off any damaged branches beyond repair and arbor-tie any leaning branches to prevent further damage and restore strength. Look for torn and peeled bark on trees and shrubs from winter winds. Use a sharp knife to smooth the area as much as possible to prevent moisture accumulation and future hiding places for insects. Once repaired, the branch will start to form new tissue and heal itself. Note: There has been much controversy over the usage of sealants. Recent studies have concluded that wound sealants may hinder healing by allowing moisture retention, leading to possible fungal infection, so it is better to allow natural healing.

Indoors, start sowing seeds for your vegetable garden. Use biodegradable peat pots, so that the entire plant and pot can be transferred to the garden. You can also use cleaned eggshells with a little potting soil as starter pots. The eggshells will biodegrade when planted, adding valuable calcium to the soil. Plan your edible garden carefully. Onions should be planted alongside beets, carrots, dill, lettuce, and tomatoes, but should not be planted near peas, beans, or asparagus, as they will stunt the growth of these plants.

Later in the month, once the threat of frost has passed, cut back tender perennials such as Liriope and ornamental grasses and remove any winter damaged foliage from semi-evergreen varieties of heuchera and sedge. Once the chores are done, sit back, relax, and enjoy all those glorious spring blooms!

~MARCH~

ERANTHIS HYEMALIS (WINTER ACONITE)

Blooming before crocus, Winter Aconite displays bright yellow buttercup like flowers on a 3-6 inch tall by wide plant. Hardy in USDA zones 4-9, Eranthis Hyemalis prefers a location with partial to full shade and moderate watering, especially during bloom. Plant tubers two to three inches deep in late summer to early fall to enjoy early blooms that poke through the snow. These plants can be tricky to get started; however, are extremely low maintenance and will spread naturally once established. Winter Aconite serves well in mass plantings, rock gardens or naturalized in woodland and wildflower areas and is deer and rodent resistant, as all parts of the plant, especially the tubers, are poisonous if ingested. Although the taste is a deterrent, do take extra caution when planting around small children or pets. As with other tubers, allow foliage to die back completely before removing.

CROCUS VERNUS (SPRING BLOOMING CROCUS)

One of the first signs that spring has arrived is the sighting of crocus. Crocus is a member of the iris family, growing from underground roots called corms and ranging in a variety of colors from yellow to purple, white and variegated forms. Crocus hardiness varies slightly depending on which type you are growing and exposure, but most are reliable within USDA hardiness zones 3 to 8. While providing late winter-early spring interest, corms tend to naturalize for an even larger and more beautiful display year after year. They bloom and survive best where winters are cold and require a 12 to 15-week period of colder temperatures to set their blooms. Plant crocus in fall (October-November) in an area of full sun and a well-drained slightly acidic soil. If squirrels are a problem, cover your planting bed with a thin layer of wire mesh to ensure their survival. When the flowers are spent, allow the foliage to die back naturally so that the bulbs can produce food for the following year.

HELLEBORUS 'DARK AND HANDSOME' (LENTEN ROSE)

Helleborus 'Dark and Handsome' is one of the first and most dramatic blooms of spring, displaying evergreen leathery foliage with large double flower petals ranging in hues of deep purple to tuxedo black. Hardy in USDA zones 4-9, this variety grows to a height and width of 18-24 inches. Plant Helleborus Dark and Handsome in a location with partial to full shade (northern or northeastern exposure) and a moderately moist well-drained soil. This variety is part of the Helleborus Wedding Party series and is often used in bridal bouquets and boutonnieres due to its exquisite color. Helpful Tip: In locations with colder winters, it is helpful to spray the foliage of Hellebores with an anti-desiccant in autumn when daytime temperatures are dropping down into the 40's and 50's. Hellebores are perennials, but they are also broad-leaved evergreens. Anti-desiccant can help to prevent moisture loss from foliage, while keeping those leaves looking nice and healthy!

HELLEBORUS HGC 'CHAMPION' (LENTEN ROSE)

Helleborus 'Champion' is another variety of Lenten Rose that starts its blooms a little later in the season and lasts well into

April. Hardy in USDA zones 5-8, 'Champion' produces pink buds that open to voluminous white flowers on evergreen leathery foliage. As blooms age they turn to a softer greenish hue with pink highlights. Like other members of the Helleborus genus, plant 'Champion' in a location with full to partial shade and moderate watering and enjoy its blooms through spring! This perennial is also deer resistant.

HYACINTH ORIENTALIS (DUTCH HYACINTH)

Known for their highly fragrant blooms, Hyacinth Orientalis, also known as Common Hyacinth or Dutch Hyacinth, are hardy in USDA zones 4-8, and come in a variety of colors ranging from white to cream, pink, apricot, cobalt blue, deep purple and yellow. Native to southwestern Asia, southern and central Turkey, Syria, Lebanon and Israel, this popular bulbous perennial came to Europe in the 16th century and is now widely

GARDENING BY MONTH

grown in the Netherlands. It has become a well-known addition to the landscape worldwide. Bulbs produce a dense, compact spike of blooms ranging 6 to 12 inches in height that last for weeks. Hyacinth bulbs need a cooling period of 12-14 weeks with temperatures of 40 to 45-degrees Fahrenheit to bloom properly. Plant Hyacinth bulbs in the fall in a location with full sun and a loose, well-drained soil. After blooming, snip faded flowers, but allow the foliage to die back naturally before removing. Hyacinths are deer resistant.

NARCISSUS (DAFFODIL)

Daffodils (Narcissus pseudonarcissus) are spring blooming perennials in the amaryllis family, Amaryllidaceae. The daffodil is looked upon as an icon of new beginnings and rebirth and symbolizes the beginning of spring. The Latin name for daffodil is Narcissus, believed to be named after the son of the river god from Greek mythology. Their attractive flowers usually bear showy yellow or white flowers with six petals and a trumpet-shape central corona. Daffodils are perfect for planting between shrubs or in a perennial border and look wonderful naturalized in a woodland garden. Plant daffodil bulbs in Fall (October-November) in a location with full sun and a well-drained soil. Lovely yellow-white blooms appear on long stems in early spring. Most Daffodils are hardy in USDA zones 3-8 and require a cold period to set blooms. Daffodils are both deer resistant and rodent proof, as these animals do not like the taste of bulbs in the Narcissus family.

FORTHYSIA INTERMEDIA 'LYNWOOD' (BORDER FORTHYSIA)

Forthysia is an arching deciduous shrub known for its abundance of bright yellow blooms in late winter and early spring. Hardy in USDA zones 5-8, this shrub grows to a height and width of 6 to 9 feet high by wide and bears medium green leaves that turn purplish in fall. Plant Forthysia in a location with full sun to partial shade and moderate watering and prune as needed after blooming in spring.

CHAENOMELES SPECIOSA (FLOWERING QUINCE)

Chaenomeles speciosa, also known as Flowering Quince, is a genus of flowering shrub in the family Rosaceae, known for its spectacular display of pinkish-red blooms in early to late spring, which are excellent in cut flower arrangements. This attractive deciduous shrub matures to a height and width of 4-5 feet tall by 3-4 feet wide and prefers to be planted in a location with full to partial sun in a moderately moist, yet well-drained soil. Hardy in USDA zones 5-9, Flowering Quince is extremely drought tolerant and a survivalist in the most extreme of climates. While many varieties have thorns, this variety Double Take 'Pink Storm' is thornless and does not produce fruit. Chaenomeles speciosa is also deer resistant.

WEEPING PUSSY WILLOW (SALIX CAPREA PENDULA)

Hardy in USDA zones 4-8, Salix caprea 'Pendula' is a beautiful addition to the landscape with its characteristic pendulous branches that resemble a living umbrella and production of fluffy silvery-white catkins that form in early spring. Weeping

Pussy Willow reaches a mature height and width of approximately 6-8 feet tall by 4-5 feet wide and prefers a location with full sun and a moderately moist to wet soil. Under ideal conditions, this tree can be expected to live for 40 years or more. This willow is not particular to soil type or pH and is highly tolerant of urban pollution. It is even known to thrive in inner city environments.

Catkins form on the growth of the previous season and open to expose yellow pollen bearing stamens, so pruning should be performed after the bloom.

GARDENING BY MONTH

Chapter 4: The April Garden

As April arrives, the gardening season is underway. Perennials such as Hosta, liriope, chrysanthemum, Montauk Daisy, and daylily can be dug and divided as soon as they break dormancy when foliage just emerges. Use a sharp spade to dig around the drip line and lift the clumps. Break them into smaller sections, each having three to five vigorous roots, and plant right away. Keep the divided plants watered to allow the roots to become established. There are some perennials that prefer being divided in the late summer instead of early spring. These include peony, lily, garden phlox, poppies, and bearded iris. A general rule of thumb is to divide perennials that flower between early spring and mid-June in early fall, while perennials that flower after mid-June are best divided in the spring.

Early spring is the time to prune and fertilize your roses. The best time to proceed is after the last frost date when your plants are dormant or just pushing out new growth. Prune back one third of the way and cut out any dead or broken branches to return strength back to the plant. If you are unsure about a branch being alive, gently scrape the bark until you view green underneath. It the layer underlying the bark is not green, the branch is no longer viable, and should be pruned. In the case of Knock Out Roses, Carpet Roses and Drift Roses, I prune back regularly during the growing season to keep the plants full and compact and promote more blooms. Non-flowering evergreens are best pruned now before new growth.

Certain acid-loving plants such as azalea, rhododendron, magnolia, dogwood, and hydrangea prefer a soil pH between 4.5-6.0. Test surrounding soil in April and apply elemental sulfur (approximately one and a half pounds per 100 square feet or one ounce per plant) as needed. This practice will keep your flowering trees and shrubs healthy and looking their best.

~APRIL~

MAGNOLIA STELLATA 'ROYAL STAR'

The month of April brings Magnolia blooms. Magnolia stellata 'Royal Star' is a highly cold tolerant Magnolia with a shrubby oval habit reaching 10-15 feet in height by 10-12 feet wide. In early spring before leaves emerge, the tree is covered in large, fragrant, creamy white flowers that resemble stars. This is usually the first star magnolia to begin flowering, and its neat upright habit makes it very desirable for smaller spaces. Magnolia 'Royal Star' is hardy in USDA zones 4-8 and prefers a location in full sun to partial shade and a moderately moist, but well-drained soil. In autumn the interest continues as the tree's medium-green foliage turns to a bright yellow and buds develop for the following season. Growth rate of this tree is moderate.

GARDENING BY MONTH

PRUNUS CERASIFERA 'KRAUTER VESUVIUS'
(FLOWERING PLUM)

Prunus cerasifera 'Krauter Vesuvius' is a medium-sized, round-headed deciduous tree with some of the darkest purple leaves known, which continue into fall. Hardy in USDA zones 5-8, this ornamental tree produces a profusion of showy light pink blossoms in early spring, followed by small edible fruits late summer into autumn, which are an attraction to birds. Flowering Plum reaches a mature size of 15-20 feet high by wide and prefers to be planted in a location with full sun, moderate watering, and a well-drained soil.

GARDENING BY MONTH

Foliage remains a deep burgundy and lasts well into autumn, continuing interest throughout the remainder of the season. Another variety of Flowering Plum popular in the landscape is Prunus cerasifera 'Thundercloud'. Both species are similar, only the foliage of 'Krauter Vesuvius' is darker.

GARDENING BY MONTH

MUSCARI ARMENICUM (GRAPE HYACINTH)
PHOTO CREDIT: OPIOLA JERZY WIKIMEDIA COMMONS

Hardy in USDA zones 3-9, Muscari armenicum, commonly known as Grape Hyacinth, is a spring blooming perennial bulb in the family Liliaceae. Clusters of mildly fragrant deep blue-purple flowers resembling grapes appear in early spring on six to eight-inch-tall stalks with each stalk containing twenty to forty flowers. Blooms start opening from bottom up producing an ongoing display. Grape Hyacinth serve best naturalized in mass plantings as in garden borders and rock gardens. Bulbs should be planted in the fall in a location with full sun to partial shade in a well-drained soil. After flowering, allow the grass-like foliage of this perennial to die back naturally before removing. Muscari, armenicum is considered deer resistant.

**CONVALLARIA MAJALIS (LILY OF THE VALLEY)
PHOTO CREDIT: H. ZELL WIKIPEDIA**

Considered one of the most popular of the "old fashioned" perennials, Convallaria majalis, or Lilly of the Valley, is a woodland flowering plant hardy in USDA zones 3-8. This herbaceous perennial is a favorite for growing as a groundcover in semi-shady areas such as in woodland gardens or as an understory planting. Plant Lilly of the Valley in a location with full sun to partial shade and moderately moist soil. Convallaria majalis forms clumps of large green foliage while displaying spikes of sweetly scented bell-shaped blooms. Plants grow to a mature size of 6-12 inches tall by 12-24 inches wide that spread quickly by rhizomes. All parts of Lily of the Valley can be potentially dangerous to humans and animals. It is deer resistant and often used as a groundcover substitute for Hosta.

GARDENING BY MONTH

TULIPA (TULIP)

Tulips are a genus of spring blooming bulb in the family Liliaceae. Originally found as a wildflower growing in central Asia, tulips were cultivated for pleasure in Turkey as far back as 1000 AD. In 1593, Dutch botanist and professor Carolus Clusius who studied exotic plants, arrived in the Netherlands bringing tulip bulbs given to him by a friend for the purpose of establishing an experimental botanical garden at the University of Leiden. He carefully studied the different traits of tulips as he cultivated them, and his garden became increasingly popular, especially during springtime when the tulips were blooming. In 1596 and again in 1598, some of Clusius's tulips were stolen from the garden and tulip gardens started showing up all throughout the Netherlands. They rapidly became one of the country's most prized crops.

Tulips are mostly hardy in USDA zones 4-7 and prefer an area of full sun and a well-drained soil. They requre of period of cold to be able to bloom in consecutive years, so in warmer climates (zones 8-10) refrigerating the bulbs for 6-8 weeks before planting will help to produce blooms. Tulips are associated with different meanings. Red tulips are strongly associated with true love while white symbolizes royalty and yellow promotes happiness and sunshine.

PHLOX SUBULATA (CREEPING PHLOX)

Creeping or groundcover phlox is a popular herbaceous perennial, forming a carpet of colorful slightly fragrant blooms in mid-late spring. Hardy in USDA zones 3-8, this perennial grows to a height and width of 4-6 inches tall by 12-18 inches wide and prefers a location with full sun and a moderately moist, well-drained soil. Creeping Phlox is best suited for rock gardens, slopes, cascading over walls and perennial borders. Depending on the species, blooms range from white to pink, rose, lavender and magenta. Creeping phlox is relatively low maintenance and does not require deadheading but may be sheared after bloom to make for a tidier plant and in some cases promote a second bloom. This perennial is also hummingbird and butterfly friendly.

PIERIS JAPONICA 'CAVATINE' (DWARF JAPANESE ANDROMEDA)

Hardy in USDA zones 4-8, Dwarf Japanese Andromeda 'Cavatine' is a compact 18 to 24-inch high by 24-30-inch-wide evergreen shrub displaying year-round interest. Bell-shaped, creamy white blooms appear in early spring covering the entire plant, which contrast nicely against dark green foliage. Also known as Dwarf lily-of-the-valley shrub, this cultivar makes a beautiful low informal statement in the garden. Other varieties of Japanese Andromeda include, but are not limited to, 'Dorothy Wycoff' (hardy in USDA zones 4-7 and reaching 4 to 6 feet tall by 4 to 5 feet wide), 'Mountain Fire' (hardy in USDA zones 4-7 and growing to 8 to 10 feet high by 6 to 8 feet wide), and 'Forest Flame' (hardy in USDA zones 5-9 and growing to 4 to 7 feet tall by wide). All three are also known for their changing foliage in spring and fall. Another variety, 'Katsura', hardy in USDA zones 6-8 and growing to 4 to 5 feet tall by wide, is known for its newly formed deep wine-red foliage which emerges after blooms in early summer. Plant Japanese Andromeda in partial to full shade in a moderately moist soil. Allow soil to stay moist, but not overly wet or dry, as this plant will not tolerate extreme conditions. Pieris japonica blooms on the previous year's growth; therefore, pruning should be performed once the flowers fade in late April. Japanese Andromeda is known to be deer resistant.

Varieties of Pieris japonica offer autumn interest as well. Seen here on Pieris 'Cavatine' are the pink inflorescences, or clusters of showy flower buds that cover the plant from late summer into winter, while awaiting they bloom in spring, thus adding further interest to the landscape.

PULMONARIA 'MAJESTE' (LUNGWORT)

Hardy in USDA zones 4-9, Pulmonaria 'Majeste', otherwise known as Lungwort, is a herbaceous perennial that produces showy spring flowers on atractive foliage. Light pink buds open up to clusters of deep-blue bells on a 8 to 12 inch tall by 18 to 24 inch wide plant. Plant Lungwort in a location with partial to full shade and moderate watering. Plants should be cut back immediatley after blooming to rejuvenate the leaves, which will remain attractive all season. Lungwort is known to be deer resistant.

GARDENING BY MONTH

Chapter 5: The May Garden

The month of May brings an abundance of life as flowering trees, shrubs and perennials all start to shine. The landscape becomes filled with a sweet aroma and colorful blooms, that continue into the month of June as even more new interest emerges in the garden. The gardening season is well under way.

If you have not already done so, there is still time to fertilize your plants to ensure a healthy start to the season. Add a balanced all-purpose fertilizer containing nitrogen (for overall plant growth), phosphorus (for bloom production) and potassium (for healthy roots) to your evergreens, deciduous shrubs, and perennials. For certain shrubs, such as Hydrangea, the color of blooms can be altered by adding lime to raise the pH for pink blooms, aluminum sulfate to lower the pH for blue blooms, or a neutral soil can make blooms an array of blue, pink, and even purple.

To help manage the garden, edge garden beds, and continue to control weed population. A two-to-four-inch layer of organic mulch does wonders in suppressing weed growth, retaining soil moisture, and adding essential nutrients to the soil. Edibles can be moved outdoors once the threat of frost is over.

Spring flowering shrubs such as azalea, rhododendron, flowering plum or cherry, magnolia, forsythia, and lilac should be pruned now in spring after flowering, as they produce blooms on old wood. May is planting time for those summer blooming bulbs such as Dahlia, Canna, and Gladiola, which will add interest later. To ensure stronger stems and better blooms on fall blooming perennials, foliage can be pinched back on Montauk Daisies, Chrysanthemums and Asters in May and up to early July. Now, let us bring on those May blooms!

GARDENING BY MONTH

~MAY~

PRUNUS SERRULATA 'KWANZAN' (KWANZAN FLOWERING CHERRY)

Prunus serrulata, commonly known as Kwanzan Flowering Cherry is known as one of the most beautiful of the flowering ornamental trees. Hardy in USDA zones 4-8, Kwanzan Cherry is the most prolific bloomer in the flowering cherry family, displaying a profusion of vibrant double pink blossoms just before the leaves emerge in early spring. Flowers bloom in clusters of twenty to thirty petals each, providing a magnificent show in the landscape. Tree form is vase shaped with ascending branches and a spreading rounded crown. Prunus serrulata grows to a mature height and width of 20-30 feet tall by wide and prefers a location with full sun to partial shade and moderate watering. This tree is known to thrive in the most difficult of areas and is adaptable to a variety of soil types (from loamy to sandy) and soil pH's (from acidic to alkaline). After a profusion of flowers, new foliage in spring may display a bronze-red tint before turning to medium green. When autumn arrives, foliage changes from green to yellow to orange-bronze, adding further interest to the fall garden.

GARDENING BY MONTH

**CERCIS CANADENSIS (EASTERN REDBUD)
'LAVENDER TWIST'**

☀ 🜂 🦋

Cercis canadensis, commonly known as Eastern Redbud, is a deciduous flowering tree hardy in USDA zones 5-9. This weeping variety, 'Lavender Twist', is known for its contorted branches which weep towards the ground on an unusual and beautiful smaller sized tree. In spring, a profusion of lavender sweet pea-like flowers put on a show before the emergence of large heart-shaped foliage that is often tinted with purple. Foliage turns to medium green shortly after emerging, lasting through summer, then back to hues of purple, green and yellow in fall. Eastern Redbud prefers a location with full sun to part shade with moderate watering. 'Lavender Twist' reaches a height and width of 5-6 feet tall by 6-8 feet wide.

Other varieties of Eastern Redbud include 'Forest Pansy', 'Ruby Falls' and 'Hearts of Gold'. 'Forest Pansy' grows to height and width of 20-30 feet tall by 20-25 feet wide, while displaying greenish purple leaves in summer with purple undersides. 'Ruby Falls' grows 6-8 feet tall by 5-6 feet wide, displaying dark maroon foliage in summer and 'Hearts of Gold' grows 20-25 feet tall by 16-18 feet wide with foliage emerging red and turning to gold during summer while in full sun. All species of Cercis are butterfly friendly.

EVERGREEN AZALEA (GIRARD'S FUCHSIA, GIRARD'S CRIMSON AND BLAAUW'S PINK)

Hardy in USDA zones 6-9, Azalea are a group of flowering evergreen shrub belonging to the genus Rhododendron. Azaleas are available in an assortment of sizes and colors and prefer a location with full sun to partial shade and a moderately moist, well-drained soil. Azalea 'Girard's Fuchsia' produces brilliant purple-red colored blooms in mid spring and grows to a mature size of 3-4 feet tall by wide. 'Girard's Crimson' displays reddish-pink blooms in mid spring and reaches a mature size of 2-3 feet tall by wide. 'Blaauw's Pink' produces salmon-pink blooms in mid to late spring and grows to a mature size of 3-5 feet tall by wide. Other varieties include the Encore and Bloom-A-Thon series, both newer re-blooming cultivars, producing blooms in spring and then again in late summer to autumn. A smaller, more compact variety is Azalea 'Gumpo', available in pink or white and reaching a height and width of 12-24 inches tall by 3-5 feet wide. 'Gumpo' blooms in late spring. Azaleas are butterfly and hummingbird friendly.

IRIS SIBIRICA 'PANSY PURPLE' (SIBERIAN IRIS)

Siberian Iris, hardy in USDA zones 4-9 are a popular addition to the spring garden. This variety displays deep purple blooms that last for weeks on top of 24 to 36-inch-tall stalks. Siberian Iris are sold mostly as bulbs and are available in an assortment of colors including blue, pink, yellow and white. Plant this perennial in full sun to partial shade and give it moderate watering and space to grow. Clumps spread by rhizomes and will mass together to eliminate weeds. This perennial is not preferred by deer.

IRIS GERMANICA (TALL BEARDED IRIS)

Hardy in USDA zones 3-9, Iris germanica, or Tall Bearded Iris, are known for their glorious blooms in spring on a 2 to 3 foot tall by 1 to 2-foot-wide plant with deep green, sword-shaped foliage. This herbaceous perennial spreads by underground rhizomes and flowers range in color from purple to violet, blue, lavender, yellow, peach, white, and multi-colored. Plant iris in a location with full sun and moderate watering. Remove spent bloom stalks after flowering and allow the foliage to die completely back in autumn before removing. Divide your iris every few years to rejuvenate. As with other iris, Bearded Iris are not preferred by deer, but they have been known to nibble on the foliage early in the season when food availability is low. Hummingbirds are attracted to the nectar rich blooms.

GARDENING BY MONTH

ALLIUM GIGANTEUM 'GLOBEMASTER'
(ORNAMENTAL ONION)

Allium 'Globemaster' has become one of my favorite spring conversation pieces in the garden. Hardy in USDA zones 4-8, Allium 'Globemaster' displays massive four to six-inch round (or larger) lavender-purple blooms composed of small, star-shaped florets, that bloom for weeks. This bulbous perennial reaches a height and width of 3 to 4 feet tall by 9 to 12 inches wide and prefers full sun, moderate watering, and a well-drained soil. It is drought tolerant once established. After the blooms fade, the star-like seed heads rising above tall sturdy stems continue to add interest to the garden. HELPFUL TIP: Plant Allium bulbs in Fall between perennials with clumping foliage, such as Daylily 'Stella D Oro'. The deep green basal leaves that appear in spring fade as the season progresses and the foliage of the daylily will provide a fuller look at the base of your plants. Deer find this perennial to be undesirable.

ALLIUM 'MONT BLANC' (ORNAMENTAL ONION)

Allium 'Mont Blanc', another stunning variety of Allium, displays large creamy white two to four-inch blooms that also last for weeks at a time, rising above sturdy upright 3 to 4-foot-high stems. Hardy in USDA zones 4-8, Allium 'Mont Blanc' prefers a location with full sun, moderate watering, and a well-drained soil. This perennial is not desired by deer and is drought tolerant once established. This cultivar of allium, as with others, are perfect for massing and xeriscaping and the white variety makes the perfect addition to a moon garden! Other varieties of ornamental onion include, but are not limited to, Allium giganteum 'Gladiator' (lavender-blue, 3-4' tall), Allium aflatuence 'Purple Sensation' (deep purple, 2-3' tall), Allium christophii (pinkish-purple, 12-18" tall) and Allium stipitatum 'Mount Everest' (white, 3-4' tall).

SALVIA NEMEROSA 'MAY NIGHT' (PERENNIAL SAGE)

Perennial sages are a beautiful addition to any summer garden and come in a variety of cultivars ranging from 18-24 inches to 2-3 feet in height. A favorite for long bloom time and vibrant color is Salvia nemerosa 'May Night'. This lovely perennial is deer resistant and an attraction to both butterflies and hummingbirds. Salvia 'May Night' displays deep purple blooms from late May through July on 12 to18 inch spikes and is hardy in USDA Zone 3-9. Salvia prefer to be grown in full sun in a moist, yet well-drained soil and are drought tolerant once established. With regular pinching back of spent blooms, this beautiful perennial can have a repeat performance all the way through fall. Salvia is easy to propagate through stem cuttings or division of a mature plant. The best time to divide is in early spring when new foliage just starts to appear. It is recommended to apply a layer of mulch around the new planting and keep it well watered until established. A balanced fertilizer (10-10-10 or 20-20-20) in springtime on established plants will help to promote fuller green foliage and vibrant blooms.

ITOH PEONY 'BARTZELLA'

After many years of experimentation, Japanese horticulturist, Dr. Toichi Itoh, successfully created seven peony hybrids from a tree peony in 1948, which were known to become the first Itoh peonies. Members of this cultivar have large, long lasting blooms and strong stems that do not require staking. Hardy in USDA zones 4-9, 'Bartzella' produces voluminous yellow blooms that appear in late May and last for several weeks. After bloom, the deeply lobed dark green foliage on a 3-4 foot-high by wide plant lasts all summer and into fall, making an attractive addition to the garden. Plant Itoh peonies in full sun to partial shade in a rich, well-drained soil and feed in spring with a low nitrogen fertilizer to promote blooms. Once blooms have completed in late spring, Itoh peony can be deadheaded by removing spent flower stalks, leaving its attractive foliage to remain. In autumn, once the foliage turns brown, cut back plants to soil level. (Note: In warmer climates, such as USDA hardiness zones 8-9, where growth buds can survive the winter, stems can be left at 4-6 inches above ground.) In colder climates, it is recommended to mulch around the plant to insulate the roots from freezing temperatures. Itoh peonies are also known to be more disease resistant and are not preferred by deer.

PAEONIA 'KARL ROSENFELD' (DOUBLE PEONY)

Paeonia 'Karl Rosenfeld' is another hardy selection of peony with stronger stems that do not require staking. 'Karl Rosenfeld' is hardy in USDA zones 3-8 and produces brilliant fuchsia double blooms in late spring that are slightly fragrant. This deciduous perennial grows to a height and width of 30-36 inches and refers a location with full sun to partial shade and a moderately moist, well-drained soil. 'Karl Rosenfeld' is deer resistant and has the same maintenance requirements as other peonies.

RHODODENDRON CATAWBIENSE 'ROSEUM ELEGANS'

Hardy in USDA zones 4-8, Rhododendron 'Roseum Elegans' produces clusters of lilac purple trumpet shaped blooms in mid-late spring on evergreen foliage. 'Roseum Elegans' grows to a mature height and width of 8 to 10 feet tall by 6 to 10 feet wide and grows best in full sun to partial shade in an acidic, moderately moist, yet well-drained soil. There are a variety of Rhododendron to choose from, each varying in color and mature size. Excellent companion shrubs for Rhododendron include Azalea and Spirea. The trumpet shaped blooms of Rhododendron are an attraction to hummingbirds!

SYRINGA VULGARIS (LILAC) PHOTO CREDIT: MARISA DEMEGLIO WIKIPEDIA

Hardy in USDA zones 3-7, Syringa vulgaris, otherwise known as the popular Common Lilac, produces panicles of highly fragrant purple, lavender, white, or pink blooms that last for weeks on an 8-15 foot tall by 6-12-foot-wide deciduous shrub. Another smaller cultivar, Syringa 'Penda' (Bloomerang Lilac) is known for its production of blooms totaling months rather than weeks. Blooms start in spring on a 4-5 foot tall by wide shrub, then appear again later in summer after a rest period. Lilac set buds for the following season shortly after bloom. Plant in a location with full sun and moderate watering and prune immediately after flowering. Syringa vulgaris are an attraction to butterflies.

SYRINGA PATULA 'MISS KIM' (KOREAN LILAC)

Syringa patula 'Miss Kim' displays a more compact rounded, habit when compared to the traditional Common Lilac, making it a more convenient fit for smaller spaces. 'Miss Kim' grows to a mature size of 6 to 8 feet tall by wide and prefers to be grown in a location with full sun and moderate watering. Dark purple buds open to highly fragrant panicles of pale purple blooms in spring that last for weeks, followed by foliage that turns to an attractive purplish red to maroon in fall. As with other members of the Syringa family, the following year's buds set shortly after flowering, so prune immediately after bloom. 'Miss Kim' Lilac is an attraction to both butterflies and hummingbirds.

GARDENING BY MONTH

AJUGA REPTANS 'BURGUNDY GLOW' (BUGLEWEED)

Ajuga or Bugleweed is a quick growing, easy to maintain groundcover, which is excellent when planted in shady locations where other plants may have difficulty. Hardy in USDA zones 3-9, Ajuga 'Burgundy Glow' is one of the most popular varieties of Ajuga, known for its low mounding foliage which is dappled in hues of green, creamy white and smoky pink to burgundy. Spikes of blue-purple flowers appear in mid-spring to early summer on a 4-6 inch-tall by 12-18-inch-wide plant. 'Burgundy Glow' is excellent as a groundcover in smaller areas. If you are looking to cover a larger area, selecting either a bronze or green-leaved variety, such as 'Catlin's Giant' is recommended. Plant Ajuga in full sun to full shade in a location with moderate watering. Ajuga is butterfly friendly and deer resistant.

DICENTRA SPECTABILIS (OLD FASHIONED BLEEDING HEART)

Dicenta spectabilis, Old-Fashioned Bleeding Heart, is one of the oldest and most popular perennials in cultivation in the spring garden. Dangling pink heart-shaped blooms with white highlights appear on arching stems that rise above a mound of upright foliage that somewhat resembles ferns. Hardy in USDA zones 3-9, Dicentra thrives best in partial to full shade in a rich organic soil with moderate watering. Bleeding Heart is a wonderful addition to the woodland garden and is also deer resistant. This perennial has recently been recognized by a distinct genus and species and is still known as Dicentra spectabilis, but can also be listed as Lamprocapnos spectabilis.

GARDENING BY MONTH

DIANTHUS EVERLAST 'LAVENDER + EYE' (GARDEN PINKS)

Hardy in USDA zones 4-9, this hybrid strain of Dianthus, or Garden Pinks, is the perfect plant for the perennial border, rock garden or mixed container. Fragrant, re-blooming lavender-pink blooms with fringed petals appear above clumping blue-green foliage that reaches a height and width of 8-12 inches tall by 10-14 inches wide. Dianthus prefers a location with full sun to partial shade in a moderately moist, well-drained soil. Remove faded flowers to maximize bloom. These perennials are deer resistant and an attraction to hummingbirds and butterflies. Other varieties of Dianthus include, but are not limited to, Dianthus 'Neon Star' (deep magenta blooms), Dianthus Everlast Orchid' (hot pink blooms) and Dianthus 'Frosty Fire' (scarlet-red blooms).

GARDENING BY MONTH

GARDENING BY MONTH

Chapter 6: The June Garden: Summer Blooms

As blooms of Kwanzan Cherry, Rhododendron, Azalea, Lilac, Peony and Salvia are underway, the display is extended into June as new blooms emerge, including those of roses, coreopsis, nepeta, viburnum, spirea and Dogwood, all now taking center stage. An array of fragrant and colorful blooms continues to grace the landscape. The month of June is not only a time of abundant blooms, it is a time to sit back and enjoy all that the garden has to offer. Certainly, there are tasks to keep your space at its best, but most of the "heavy lifting" has already been accomplished during the previous months.

June is a time for simpler routine maintenance. Deadheading spent blooms on perennials will encourage more blooms and extend their bloom season. Some perennials that benefit from deadheading include salvia, dianthus, and daylily. Prune spring flowering shrubs after bloom and continue to feed your roses monthly with an all-in-one fertilizer and systemic fungicide to keep them healthy. Prune roses if desired to maintain fuller plants and deadhead spent flowers to encourage further blooms. If non-flowering evergreens need further pruning after their flush of spring growth, prune slightly to shape. Additionally, keep up the weeding. The proactive removal of a few weeds now will prevent further spread and much more effort later. If you have not yet applied a layering of organic mulch to your garden beds, it is still a good time to do so, for it will assist in keeping those weeds under control!

If you are growing edibles, June is a good time to plant tender vegetables such as basil, carrots, radishes and beets and to pinch back side shoots on tomatoes. Pinching encourages stronger plants with larger juicier fruit, which will be appreciated later. Watering is crucial once the temperatures start to rise. Generally, garden plantings should receive approximately one inch of water per week. Watering when it is cooler during early morning or late afternoon hours is best.

~JUNE~

ROSA 'RADTKOPINK' (PINK DOUBLE KNOCK OUT ROSE)

Roses are a wonderful way to welcome June. Hardy in USDA zones 5-10, the Knock-Out Family of Roses are the easiest to grow and most disease resistant of the roses. Blooms appear in late spring and last well into fall on this re-blooming shrub that just keeps on giving. This variety, Pink Double Knock Out, produces gorgeous double pink blooms on a 3-4 foot tall by wide deciduous shrub. Plant Knock Out Roses in full sun and water from the roots for best results. This cultivar requires no dead heading but I find that regular pruning keeps the plant more compact and encourages more blooms. I would also recommend feeding your roses monthly with a systemic granular fertilizer and fungicide all in one, which is simply scattered along the base of the plant. Other varieties of Knock

Out Rose include, but are not limited to, Rosa 'Radrazz' (single red blooms), Rosa 'Radtko' (double red blooms) and Rosa 'Radsunny' (yellow blooms).

ROSA 'MEISWETDOM' (SWEET DRIFT ROSE)

Hardy in USDA zones 4-11, Drift Rose, a cross between the full size and miniature rose, are repeat bloomers and available in a multitude of colors ranging from pink to apricot, peach coral, red, yellow, and white. This cultivar is exceptionally disease resistant, making it easy to grow and maintain and grows to a mature size of just 12-18 inches tall by 24-30 inches wide. Other favorites in the Drift Rose series include, but or not limited to, Rosa 'Meimirrote' (Apricot Drift Rose), Rosa 'Meiggili' (Peach Drift Rose), Rosa 'Meidrifora' (Coral Drift Rose), Rosa 'Meigalpio' (Red Drift Rose) and Rosa 'Novarospop' (Popcorn Drift Rose). Plant Drift Rose in full sun, and as with other roses, watering from the roots is best.

GARDENING BY MONTH

VIBURNUM PLICATUM TOMENTOSUM 'SUMMER SNOWFLAKE'

Viburnum 'Summer Snowflake', also known as Doublefile Viburnum, is hardy in USDA zones 5-8, producing clusters of delicate snowflake-like blooms late spring into early summer on a dense, multi-stemmed deciduous shrub. 'Summer Snowflake' grows to a height and width of 5-8 feet tall by 8-10 feet wide and requires full sun to partial shade and a moist, well-drained soil. Following the bloom cycle, fertile blossoms may turn into bright red fruits that deepen to black and are a summer treat for birds. Throughout the rest of the season, blooming appears sporadically, and just as other plants are going dormant, 'Summer Snowflake' brings yet another round of interest to the landscape. The medium to dark green foliage turns to a burgundy, purplish red as the fall season progresses. This shrub is moderately deer resistant, low maintenance and is not prone to any serious insect or disease problems. To maintain a more compact shrub, prune after flowering.

GARDENING BY MONTH

WEIGELA FLORIDA 'SPILLED WINE'

Weigela florida 'Spilled Wine' is a flowering shrub prized for its deep burgundy foliage and magenta blooms that appear in late spring. 'Spilled Wine' is hardy in USDA zones 4-8 and grows to a mature size of 2-3 feet tall by 3-4 feet wide, making it perfect for small spaces. Weigela prefers a location with full sun, moderate watering and is an attraction to hummingbirds and butterflies. Other cultivars of Weigela include, but are not limited to, Weigela 'My Monet', 'Dark Horse' and 'Wine & Roses'. 'My Monet' is hardy in USDA zones 4-6, grows to a mature size of 12-18 inches tall by 18-24 inches wide and displays green, white, and pink variegated foliage. 'Dark Horse' is hardy in USDA zones 4-8, grows 2-3 feet tall by wide and displays darker purple-black foliage. 'Wine & Roses', hardy in USDA zones 4-8, grows to a height and width of 4-5 feet and displays dark green foliage with burgundy highlights. Weigela is listed as moderately deer resistant, but from experience, I have seen them nibble on the foliage of new plants.

WISTERIA FLORIBUNDA (JAPANESE WISTERIA)

Wisteria floribunda is a hardy deciduous twiner that can be grown on a strong support or as a tree form as shown. Long hanging clusters of fragrant pea-like blooms cover the tree in late spring, followed by bright green pinnate shaped leaves and hanging velvety seed pods that persist into autumn. Japanese Wisteria is hardy in USDA zones 4-9, blooms on old wood and prefers a location with full sun and moderate watering. Bloom colors range depending on the cultivar and can be seen in shades of lavender, pink, blue, or white. Tree form size ranges from 10-25 feet tall by 4-8 feet wide. Wisteria sinensis, or Chinese Wisteria produces blue-violet blooms in May-June and is hardy in USDA zones 5-8. Chinese and Japanese Wisteria are considered invasive in the Midwest and should not be planted in those areas. A native, non-invasive form of Wisteria (Wisteria frutescens or American Wisteria) produces lilac-purple blooms in April-May and is hardy in USDA zones 5-9. Wisteria is not preferred by deer.

PRUNUS LAUROCERASUS 'OTTO LUYKEN' (CHERRY LAUREL)

Hardy in USDA zones 6-8, Prunus laurocerasus 'Otto Luyken', or Cherry Laurel, is not only an attractive broad-leaved evergreen, but it also produces spikes of creamy white blooms in mid-late spring, that may repeat in fall. This compact 3 to 4 foot tall by 6 to 8-foot-wide shrub prefers a location with full sun to partial shade, and a moderately moist soil with good drainage, as it does not like its roots to be constantly wet. Little maintenance is needed with this hardy shrub but do check regularly for insect or fungal damage. As with other broad-leaved evergreens, spraying with an anti-desiccant in late fall is recommended. (See Chapter 12: Care of Broad-leaved Evergreens.) To keep a more compact shrub, prune after the rush of new foliage and blooms in spring. Growing to 8 to 10 feet in height, Skip Laurel is a taller cultivar of Prunus laurocerasus. Cherry and Skip Laurel are not preferred by deer.

PRUNUS SUBHIRTELLA 'PENDULA' (WEEPING FLOWERING CHERRY)

Known as one of the most popular weeping trees in the landscape, Weeping Flowering Cherry is known for its magnificent display of light pink or white blooms in late spring, cascading from graceful branches, which can reach the ground. Prunus subhirtella 'Pendula', hardy in USDA zones 5-8, is a medium sized deciduous tree which prefers a location with full sun and low to moderate watering. Prunus subhirtella grows to a mature height and width of 15-20 feet high by wide. This beauty makes the perfect specimen tree for a front lawn or island bed. Another variety of Weeping Cherry with a smaller stature and white blooms is Prunus 'Snofozam', or Weeping Snow Fountain Cherry. Weeping Snow Fountain Cherry grows to a mature height and width of 8-15 feet high by 6-8 feet wide. Weeping Cherry is drought tolerant once established.

GARDENING BY MONTH

CORNUS 'KOUSA' (JAPANESE KOUSA DOGWOOD)

Kousa Dogwood, hardy in USDA zones 5-8, is one of the hardier and more disease resistant cultivars of Dogwood. This small, deciduous tree is known for its display of beautiful large white blooms that appear in late spring to early summer, on a background of deep green, oval shaped foliage. Displaying a rounded canopy and branches horizontally layered in tiers, Kousa Dogwood reaches a mature height and width of 15-30 feet tall by wide. Blooms are composed of four showy bracts surrounding a central cluster of smaller, less conspicuous flowers.

In late summer, attractive round, red fruits appear that ripen in fall and are edible by both birds and humans. Autumn foliage turns to a reddish-purple and bark is mottled in shades of tan, gray, and brown. Plant Kousa Dogwood in a location with full to partial sun with moderate watering and a well-drained soil. A newer cultivar, Cornus Kousa 'Greensleeves', has improved disease resistance and even more abundant blooms, making it an outstanding specimen tree for the landscape. Kousa Dogwood is seldom severely damaged by deer.

SPIREA JAPONICA 'MAGIC CARPET'

Spirea japonica 'Magic Carpet' belongs to a family of deciduous flowering shrubs available in numerous cultivars ranging in size and bloom color. This selection, 'Magic Carpet', is hardy in USDA zones 4-9 and grows to a mature size of 18-24 inches tall by 2-3 feet wide and produces vibrant rose-pink blooms in mid-late summer. 'Magic Carpet' is known for its wonderful display of foliage, starting off in spring with leaves that emerge as burnt red, changing to shades of bright gold and then to bronze in fall. Other varieties of Spirea include, but are not limited to, Spirea 'Little Princess' (18-30 inches tall by 2-3 feet wide, pale rose blooms and tolerates more shade), 'Anthony Waterer' (3-5 feet tall by wide with dark pink blooms) and 'Big Bang' (2-3' tall by wide, changing foliage and voluminous blooms). Two white flowering varieties include Spirea vanhouttei (5-8 feet tall by 6-10 feet wide) and 'Snowmound' (3-5 feet tall by wide). Plant Spirea in full sun in a moderately moist, well-drained soil, and prune in early spring just as foliage starts to emerge to form a compact plant and improve bloom. Spirea is both deer resistant and an attraction to pollinators.

**COREOPSIS VERTICILLATA 'ZAGREB'
(TICKSEED)**

Hardy in USDA zones 3-9, Coreopsis verticillata 'Zagreb', also known as Tickseed, is a long blooming perennial that flowers from summer and into fall. Golden yellow daisy-like flowers form on spreading clumps of very delicate, ferny foliage, creating the perfect display for a perennial border, or cutting garden. Coreopsis grows to a height and width of 12 to 18 inches and prefers a location with full sun and a well-drained soil. It is drought tolerant once established. Coreopsis' Zagreb' is an attraction to pollinators and is a welcomed addition to the deer resistant garden.

COREOPSIS 'SUNKISS' (TICKSEED)

Another variety of Coreopsis, which has been becoming increasingly popular is Coreopsis 'Sunkiss'. 'Sunkiss' is hardy in USDA zones 4-9, displaying a large burgundy center contrasting against bright yellow blooms on a 12-14 inch tall by 14-16-inch-wide plant. Shown in the photo is a combination of 'Sunkiss' Coreopsis against the bright blue evergreen foliage of Dwarf Globe Blue Spruce 'Montgomery'. Plant Coreopsis 'Sunkist' in a location with full sun and a well-drained soil. This perennial is both deer resistant and drought tolerant once established.

NEPETA 'WALKERS LOW' (CATMINT)

Hardy in USDA zones 3-8, Nepeta. also known as Catmint, is a long-blooming perennial, producing mounds of gray-green aromatic foliage and soft lavender-blue flowers from early summer through fall. This variety, 'Walkers Low' grows to a mature height and width of 2-3 feet tall by 18-24 inches wide and prefers a location with full sun to partial shade and moderate watering. Other varieties of Nepeta include, but are not limited to, Nepeta 'Blue Wonder' (deep lavender-blue blooms, 12-15 inches tall by wide), 'Junior Walker' (lavender-blue blooms, 18 inches tall by 30 inches wide) and 'Six Hills Giant' (periwinkle blue blooms, 2-3 feet tall by 15-18 inches wide). Nepeta is both deer resistant and drought tolerant once established. In this photo, the color of Nepeta is enhanced next to the foliage of Hosta Shadowland 'Autumn Frost'.

VERONICA SPICATA (SPEEDWELL)

Veronica, or Speedwell, is a herbaceous perennial, hardy in USDA zones 4-8, displaying upright spikes of purple, blue, lavender or pink blooms, depending on the variety. This cultivar, Veronica 'Royal Candles' grows to a height and width of 8-12 inches tall by 12-18 inches wide and produces deep purple-blue blooms that last all summer long, which are a major attraction to butterflies. Veronica prefers a location with full sun and moderate watering and is deer resistant. Deadhead spent blooms to extend bloom time.

HEMEROCALLIS 'STELLA D ORO' (DAYLILY)

Daylilies are a popular addition to the garden for lasting color and will bloom a long time if cared for properly. Most daylilies prefer a humus, well-drained soil in full sun but will tolerate partial shade, allowing for some flexibility when planting. There are over 80,000 cultivars of daylily with a broad range of cold hardiness from USDA zones 1-11, making them one of the most adaptable landscape plants. Out of all the daylilies, my favorite for longest bloom time is Hemerocallis 'Stella D Oro'. Developed by daylily hybridizer Walter Jablonski of

Merrillville, Indiana in 1975, this re-blooming daylily is known to have one of the longest bloom times, lasting from late spring through fall with little maintenance. Hardy in USDA zones 4-11, 'Stella D Oro' produces clumps of grassy green foliage followed by bright golden-yellow trumpet shaped blooms on 24 to 30-inch stems. To achieve re-blooms through the first frost, deadhead spent blooms before they go to seed. As greenery declines in late summer, remove any browned foliage to rejuvenate the plant. New foliage will emerge with a return of colorful blooms.

LILIUM ASIATICA (HYBRID GARDEN LILY)

The popular Asiatic Lily is a dependable bulbous perennial, hardy in USDA zones 4-9, that puts on a show in the summer garden. Lilium Asiatica grows to a height of 2-3 feet tall and is available in a variety of colors, ranging from pink to orange, red, yellow, and white, and may be purchased either as bulbs or in container. Plant Lilium in a location with full sun, moderate watering, and a well-drained soil. These perennials make excellent cut flowers. After bloom, allow the remaining green stalks to die back completely before removing in autumn.

GERANIUM 'ROZANNE' (PERENNIAL GERANIUM/CRANESBILL)

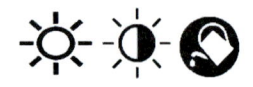

Perennial Geranium is an excellent addition to the garden border, rock garden or container. Hardy in USDA zones 4-8, Geranium 'Rozanne' forms a mound of green star-like foliage with cup shaped bright blue-violet flowers that appear in early to mid-summer. Plant this perennial in a location with full sun to partial shade and provide moderate watering. Plants grow to a height and width of 16-24 inches tall by 20-28 inches wide and bloom summer until fall. Tidy up foliage by pruning in late summer to keep plants looking full.

GARDENING BY MONTH

LEUCANTHEMUM SUPERBUM 'BANANA CREAM' (SHASTA DAISY)

Leucanthemum, or Shasta Daisy is a well-known and popular perennial selection for the sunny border. It is an attraction to butterflies and is often used in cut flower arrangements. This mid-sized selection, 'Banana Cream' displays a yellow eye surrounded by lemon yellow petals that fade to a softer yellow and eventually to ivory. Shasta Daisy 'Banana Cream' prefers a location with full to sun to part shade and moderate watering. It matures to 14-20 inches tall by 18-24 inches wide and bloom time can be increased by removing faded flowers. Another taller variety, Leucanthemum superbum 'Becky' grows to a height and width of 3-4 feet tall by 18-24 inches wide and displays large daisy like flowers with yellow centers and white petals. It exhibits excellent tolerance to heat and humidity.

GARDENING BY MONTH

ASTILBE CHINENSIS 'VISION IN RED'

Hardy in USDA zones 4-9, Astilbe is available in a range of colors and sizes, making it a welcomed perennial addition to the shade garden. This cultivar, Astilbe 'Vision in Red' produces spikes of purple-red blooms that last for weeks in mid-summer on a 12-16 inch tall by 12-18-inch-wide plant. Plant this herbaceous perennial in partial to full shade in an organically rich, moderately moist soil. The colorful blooms are an attraction to butterflies and at the end of the bloom season, seed heads are an attraction to birds. The seed heads can be left for the entire winter or pruned to the ground once completely dormant. Astilbe is listed as deer resistant, but from experience, I have seen them eat the tops off the flowers on some of the taller varieties when food sources are scarce.

GAILLARDIA (BLANKET FLOWER)

This tough, heat loving perennial displays large bright golden-orange blooms with scarlet highlights in the summer garden. Gaillardia, also known as Blanket Flower, is hardy in USDA zones 3-8 and prefers a location with full sun and low to moderate watering. Plants grow 12-18 inches tall by 12-16 inches wide and bloom continuously through fall with deadheading. Gaillardia is easy to grow and will thrive in poor, dry soils. It is both deer and drought tolerant and makes an excellent addition to a border or rock garden. This variety shown is Gaillardia 'Goblin'. Other varieties include 'Arizona Sun' (8-12 inches tall by 12-16 inches wide with darker center) and Gaillardia 'Mesa Bright Bi-Color' (16-20 inches tall by 18-24 inches wide, yellow with red center).

HEUCHERA (CORAL BELLS)

Heuchera is a low maintenance perennial known for their colorful clump forming foliage and spikes of small bell-shaped flowers in summer. Heuchera are hardy in USDA zones 4-9 and are avaialble in hues of burgundy, lime green, peachy-pink and caramel. The two varieties shown here are Heuchera villosa 'Caramel' with Heuchera micrantha 'Palace Purple' in the backdrop. I have found these two to be the better performers and will often mass them together for all season interest. Heuchera 'Caramel' is a newer semi-evergreen variety, growing 12-18 inches tall by wide, with caramel colored foliage and light pink blooms that appear later compared to other varieties. Heuchera 'Palace Purple' grows 12-24 inches tall by 12-18 inches wide with burgundy foliage and blooms that are creamy-white. Heuchera thrives best in a location with partial to full shade and moderate watering. Remove spent flower stalks in autumn and trim off any worn out foliage in spring.

GARDENING BY MONTH

CLEMATIS VITICELLA 'BONANZA' (CLIMBING CLEMATIS)

Clematis is a vigorous deciduous flowering vine that adds continuous color to the summer garden. Depending on the variety, Clematis are generally hardy in USDA zones 4-9 and come in a huge selection of colors including purple, lavender, pink, red and white and range in bloom time from spring to fall. This variety, 'Bonanza' (USDA zones 4-8) is a newer cultivar with better disease resistance, growing 8-10 feet in height by 2-3 feet wide, while producing lavender-blue blooms with pale yellow anthers from summer to early fall. Clematis requires full sun to partial shade and a fertile, well-drained soil and prefer their roots to be slightly shaded. This can be accomplished by putting a layer of mulch around the base of the plant. This climbing variety will need a support system such as a trellis to grow on. Clematis bloom on the new wood of the season. To promote flowers, deadhead spent blooms and cut back the previous year's stems to a pair of strong buds before new growth starts in spring. Clematis blooms are an attraction to hummingbirds and butterflies.

OPUNTIA HUMIFUSA (EASTERN PRICKLY PEAR CACTUS)

Prickly Pear Cactus, native to North America, could be the next conversation piece in your water wise garden. Hardy in USDA zones 4-10, large yellow cup-shaped blooms appear above fleshy pad-shaped foliage in summer, followed by deep purplish-red oblong fruit in late summer. The fruit is ripe when soft to the touch and the sweet pulp can be made into a delicious jam or jelly. Plant this drought tolerant plant in a location with full sun and low watering. The only maintenance this plant will need is to remove any spent foliage in spring.

DIGITALIS PURPUREA (COMMON FOXGLOVE)

Digitalis purpurea, or Common Foxglove is an herbaceous perennial displaying three to four-foot-high spikes of glowing rose-pink to purple bells with darker freckles on the inside, which are an attraction to both butterflies and hummingbirds. Foxglove is hardy in USDA zones 4-9 and prefers a location with full sun to partial shade and moderate watering. Digitalis purpurea is a biennial, forming clumps of coarse leaves with prominent veins the first year, followed by blooms the following season. In the second year, an additional upright stem with smaller leaves is produced above the original with spikes of flowers. Common Foxglove reproduces by seed. Pollinated flowers can produce up to 1-2 million seeds at a time that will re-seed under favorable conditions. The plant will self-sow for the following year. Deer find this perennial to be unfavorable.

GARDENING BY MONTH

GARDENING BY MONTH

Chapter 7: The July Garden

As temperatures rise, the July garden is now going into its third major stage of blooms. Hydrangea, Crape Myrtle, Lilium, Phlox, Echinacea, and Rudbeckia, to name a few, all make their debut along-side ongoing blooms from May and June. The landscape continues to be a colorful canvas with more blooms to come.

During the hotter days of summer, it is best to perform your garden chores during early morning or late day when the temperatures are more comfortable. Prune Knock Out, Carpet and Drift Roses after their first bloom cycle to maintain a compact and healthy plant and promote more blooms, while continuing to feed and apply a systemic fungicide monthly. Remove infected foliage showing brown or yellow spots from possible fungal infection and dispose of properly.

Deadhead spring blooming perennials such as salvia and dianthus to promote a second bloom, and when summer blooming perennials such as daylily, echinacea and rudbeckia come to the end of their bloom cycle, repeat the process to prolong blooms into fall. A helpful tip for prolonging the life of daylilies is to perform a partial rejuvenation in late summer. Remove faded flowers and seed stalks so that the plants energy goes back into producing new blooms. Clean up the plants appearance by removing any browned foliage, which is usually seen around its base.

If you have summer blooming annuals, they can be rejuvenated now by cutting back foliage part way in July. Adding a phosphorus-based fertilizer will help to revitalize the plant and encourage more blooms. Fall blooming perennials such as chrysanthemums and asters may be pinched back one final time.

GARDENING BY MONTH

~JULY~

**HYDRANGEA MACROPHYLLA 'BAILMER'
ENDLESS SUMMER (MOPHEAD VARIETY)**

The pride of the late summer landscape, Hydrangea is a timeless addition to the formal or informal garden, with numerous varieties to choose from, ranging in color, size, and bloom type. Hydrangea macrophylla 'Bailmer', otherwise known as 'Endless Summer Hydrangea', is a newer cultivar of re-blooming mophead hydrangea which blooms on both old and new wood, making maintenance easier. 'Endless Summer' is hardy in USDA zones 4-9, matures to 3-5 feet tall by wide, and prefers a location with partial shade and moderate watering. Blooms are pink in alkaline soils and blue in acidic soils. Removal of spent flowers will encourage further bloom. Other cultivars of re-blooming hydrangea include, but are not limited to, Hydrangea macrophylla 'Blushing Bride' (3-6 feet tall by wide and white blooms with pink blush), Hydrangea macrophylla 'BloomStruck' (3-4 feet tall by 4-5 feet wide with pink or blue blooms) and Hydrangea macrophylla 'All Summer Beauty' (3-5 feet tall by wide, with blue-violet, pink blooms).

HYDRANGEA MACROPHYLLA 'TWIST & SHOUT' (LACECAP VARIETY)

Hardy in USDA zones 4-9, Hydrangea macrophylla 'Twist & Shout' is a lacecap variety in the Endless Summer Collection. 'Twist & Shout' produces abundant lacy blooms with deep pink centers surrounded by blooms of pink or periwinkle blue, depending on soil type. 'Twist & Shout' matures to 3-5 feet tall by wide, is re-blooming, and blooms on both old and new wood. As with other hydrangea that bloom on new wood, removing spent blooms will encourage a longer bloom time. A newer more compact re-blooming lacecap variety is Hydrangea serrata 'Tuff Stuff', growing to just 2-3 feet tall by 3-4 feet wide and displaying reddish-pink flowers, which may shift to blue in acidic soils.

MONARDA 'MARSHALLS DELIGHT' (BEEBALM)

Monarda, also known as Beebalm, is hardy in USDA zones 4-9 and displays blooms throughout the summer months, which are an attraction to butterflies and hummingbirds. This traditional herbaceous perennial displays bright hot pink flowers arranged in large heads on a 30-40 inch tall by 18-30-inch-wide plant. Plant Monarda in full sun with a moderately moist, but well-drained soil, and enjoy its blooms! The foliage of 'Marshalls Delight' is fragrant and more resistant to powdery mildew than most other varieties. Additional varieties of Monarda include Monarda didyma 'Jacob Cline' (scarlet red blooms, 3-4 feet tall by 24-30 inches wide) and Monarda didyma 'Grand Parade' (purple blooms, 13-18 inches tall by 16-24 inches wide). Monarda is deer resistant.

GARDENING BY MONTH

LIGULARIA DENTATA 'OTHELLO' (LEOPARD PLANT)

Popular for shady, moist locations, Ligularia forms clusters of golden daisy-like blooms in mid-late summer that rise above clumps of rounded dark green foliage. Hardy in USDA zones 3-9, Ligularia grows to 3-4 feet tall by 18-30 inches wide and prefers a location with partial to full shade and high watering. Other varieties of Ligularia include 'Rocket' and 'Little Rocket' producing tall spires of golden-orange blooms. The leathery foliage and spiky blooms of Ligularia are not preferred by deer.

GARDENING BY MONTH

ECHINACEA PURPUREA POW WOW 'WILD BERRY' (CONEFLOWER)

For continuous blooms from mid-summer and persisting into fall, Echinacea purpurea Pow Wow 'Wild Berry' displays vibrant rosy-purple daisy-like flowers on a 16-24 inch high by 12-16-inch-wide plant. Echinacea 'Wild Berry' is hardy in USDA zones 3-9 and prefers a location with full sun and moderate watering. This herbaceous perennial serves beautifully as an addition to the perennial border, is an attraction to pollinators and the dried seed heads are an attraction to birds. In autumn, allow seed heads to remain and allow foliage to completely die back before removing. Other varieties of Echinacea include, but are not limited to, Echinacea 'Harvest Moon' (USDA zones 5-8, golden yellow blooms, 24-30 inches tall by 18-24 inches wide), Echinacea 'White Swan' (USDA zones 3-9, white blooms, 24-36 inch tall by 18-24 inches wide) and 'Cheyenne Spirit', which displays several colors on the same plant! Echinacea are rarely bothered by deer.

ECHINACEA 'CHEYENNE SPIRIT' (CONEFLOWER)

A newer hybrid form of Coneflower, 'Cheyenne Spirit', features petals in vivid shades of red, pink, rosy-purple, orange, yellow and cream all on the same plant! This cultivar has become a favorite in the perennial border and a conversation piece for passersby. Hardy in USDA zones 4-10, 'Cheyenne Spirit' grows to 24-30 inches high by 18-24 inches wide on an upright, bushy plant. Plant this herbaceous perennial in a location with full sun and moderate watering. This variety of Echinaea, as with others, is both butterfly and bird friendly. 'Cheyenne Spirit' is also known to be rarely preferred by deer.

GARDENING BY MONTH

RUDBECKIA HIRTA (BLACK-EYED SUSAN)

Rudbeckia hirta, commonly known as Black-Eyed Susan, is a North American native, hardy in USDA zones 3-9. Masses of golden daisy-like blooms surrounding a central dark brown eye appear on a 2-3 feet tall by 18-24-inch-wide plant in mid-summer. Rudbeckia prefers a location with full sun to partial shade and moderate watering and continues bloom until fall. Removing faded flowers throughout the blooming season will increase bloom time. After bloom, allow seed heads to remain, as they are a treat for birds, and allow the foliage to die back before removing. This hardy perennial spreads easily and is a good choice for mass planting. Black-eyed Susan is considered deer resistant; however, from experience I have seen deer eat off the top portion of new plants. A newer dwarf form of Black-Eyed Susan is Rudbeckia fulgida 'Little Goldstar', which displays a more compact, non-spreading habit and grows to just 14-16 inches high by wide.

GARDENING BY MONTH

ECHIBECKIA SUMMERINA 'BLAZING FIRE'

☀ 💧 🦋

Echibeckia is a new hybrid cross between Echinacea and Black-Eyed Susan, with the appearance of a Black-Eyed Susan and the vigor and disease resistance of Echinacea. Hardy in USDA zones 6-10, Echibeckia grows to a height and width of 18-24 inches tall by wide and prefers a location with full sun, moderate watering, and a well-drained soil. Allow the soil to dry out in between watering. An attraction to butterflies, bloom time is from mid-summer to fall, with blooms lasting up to two to three months.

LYTHRUM 'MORDEN'S GLEAM' (PURPLE LOOSESTRIFE)

Lythrum virgatum 'Morden's Gleam' is a seedless, non-invasive variety of Loosestrife cultivated as a cross between Lythrum 'Robert' with select forms of the North American native, Lythrum alatum. Hardy in USDA zones 4-9, this perennial grows to a height and width of 36-48 inches tall by 24 inches wide and bears beautiful tall spikes of magenta blooms in July and August that can last for several months.

Lythrum prefers to be grown in full sun in a well-drained soil, is known to be deer resistant and is an attraction to butterflies and hummingbirds. (Important Note: Lythrum is considered invasive and not for sale in some states. This "non-invasive" form may be capable of propagation if there are wild strains within proximity.)

PLATYCODON GRANDIFLORUS 'KOMACHI' (BALLOON FLOWER)

Platycodon is a species of herbaceous perennial displaying blooms that resemble inflated balloons. Hardy in USDA zones 3-8, Platycodon grows to 1-2 feet tall by 12-18 inches wide and requires a location with full sun to partial shade and moderate watering. Blooms mature as if they are going to burst, then open up into star-shaped blue flowers. This variety 'Komachi' is even more unique, in that the blooms inflate but never open. It makes a sure conversation piece in the garden. Bloom time is exceptionally long and this hardy perennial will live on for years. Other Platycodon species avaialble include, but are not limited to, 'Astra Pink' 'Astra White,' 'Fugi Pink' and 'Fugi 'White'. Platycodon is listed as deer resistant once established, but from expereince, deer have been known to nibble on new foliage, stunting the growth of the plants. Flowers still appear in late summer.

AGASTACHE 'ROSIE POSIE' ANISE HYSSOP

Agastache, otherwise known as Hyssop or Hummingbird Mint, is an herbaceous perennial hardy in USDA zones 6-9. This licorice scented member of the mint family grows to a mature size of 18-24 inch tall by 24-30 inches wide and prefers a location with full sun to partial shade with moderate watering. Agastache does require excellent drainage and is drought tolerant once established. Hot pink, blue-lavender, or orange blooms (depending on species) appear in summer on an upright clump forming plant, last for months into early fall and are an attraction to butterflies and hummingbirds. Other varieties are 'Blue Fortune' (deep blue blooms and 2-3 feet tall by 18-24 inches wide) and 'Acapulco Orange' (orange blooms and 16-18 inches tall by 18-24 inches wide). Agastache is known to be deer resistant.

LAVANDULA (LAVENDER)

Lavender is an aromatic herb which has been known for centuries to be used in perfumes, soaps, sachets, cooking and medicine. Hardy in USDA zones 5-9, fine gray-green foliage produces spikes of lavender flowers in summer that last for months. There are various forms of lavender including the species shown above, Lavendula intermedia 'Grosso' (French Lavender), Lavandula angustifolia 'Hidcote' (English Lavender) and Lavandula angustifolia 'Munstead' (English Lavender) among others. Lavender prefers a location with full sun, minimal watering and a well-drained soil, and is an attraction to butterflies. It is drought tolerant once established

GARDENING BY MONTH

and deer resistant. Size varies dependng on species, but most grow between 12-24 inches tall by wide.

ASTILBE SIMPLICIFOLIA 'SPRITE'

Astilbe 'Sprite' is a dwarf, later bloomng variety of Astilbe, whch produces feathery light pink blooms on a compact 18-24 inch tall by wide plant. Astilbe 'Sprite' prefers a location with partial to full shade and moderate watering. As seen above, the foliage and blooms of Astilbe 'Sprite' fit right into a garden border under the shade of cascading evergreens, such as Weeping White Pine. This perennial is an attraction to birds and butterflies and its compact habit and characteristic feathery blooms have proven to be deer resistant over other varieties of Astilbe.

**LILIUM ORIENTALIS 'CASA BLANCA'
(ORIENTAL LILY)**

Oriental lilies, hardy in USDA zones 4-9, are a popular addition to the garden border, known for their large highly fragrant blooms in white, pink, rose or red that appear later in summer. This variety, Lilium 'Casa Blanca' grows to a height of 2-3 feet tall and prefers a location with full sun and moderate watering. Plant bulbs in fall or purchase as an established plant in spring or summer. Lilium is long-lived, makes an excellent cut flower and is often admired in floral arrangements. The white blooms also make a nice addition to the moon garden!

LILIUM 'STARGAZER' (ORIENTAL LILY)

Worthy of its own mention, Lilium 'Stargazer' is one of the most beautiful of the Oriental Lilies. This hybrid introduced by horticulturist Leslie Woodriff in the late 1970's, displays voluminous highly fragrant crimson-pink blooms speckled with darker dots and a yellow-orange highlighted center. 'Stargazer' is hardy in USDA zones 4-9, grows 2-3 feet tall, and prefers full sun and moderate watering. It is also available in either bulb form or established plant. Mass this perennial for best effect, as it will provide years of enjoyment and become a conversation piece in the garden. After flowering, allow foliage to completely die back in fall before removing, so that bulbs can store food for the following season.

BUDDLEIA DAVIDII LO & BEHOLD 'BLUE CHIP' (DWARF BUTTERFLY BUSH)

Buddleia davidii Low & Behold 'Blue Chip', also known as dwarf Butterfly Bush, is grown for its compact, non-invasive habit and clusters of fragrant elongated purple blooms from mid-summer into fall. Hardy in USDA zones 5-9, this newer cultivar stays at a compact 2-3 feet tall by wide without pruning and prefers full sun with moderate watering. Another variety, Buddleia 'Pugster Blue' is an improved cultivar, having been taken a step further, displaying a compact habit while producing the full-sized flowers normally seen on a standard plant. These newer cultivars do not require deadheading to re-bloom, but I have found that doing so produces even more blooms and longer bloom time! The blooms of Buddleia are a major attraction to butterflies and hummingbirds. This shrub is also drought tolerant once established and deer resistant.

HYDRANGEA PANICULATA 'LITTLE LIME'

Hardy in USDA zones 3-9, Hydrangea 'Little Lime' is a new dwarf form of the popular Hydrangea 'Limelight', blooming a little later in the month than the Endless Summer Collection. Hydrangea paniculata 'Little Lime' displays beautiful delicate blooms that open as soft green, mature to creamy white then fade to pink and burgundy in the fall. This dwarf cultivar is one third the size of the traditional form of this hydrangea, only reaching a height and width of 3-5 feet tall by wide. Plant 'Little Lime' in a location with full sun to partial shade and moderate watering. Hydrangea 'Little Lime' blooms on the new wood of the season. Prune in late winter/early spring to encourage stronger stems, new growth, and more blooms.

GARDENING BY MONTH

PHLOX PANICULATA (TALL SUMMER PHLOX)

Phlox paniculata, or Summer phlox, is a popular addition to the butterfly and hummingbird friendly garden. Hardy in USDA zones 4-8, flowers in shades of lavender, violet, white, coral, pink or red (depending on the variety) appear on a 3 to 6 foot tall by 1 to 3-foot-wide plant in late summer and last into early fall. Many cultivars are fragrant, which can be even more noticeable at night. Plant Phlox in a location with full sun, moderate watering, and a well-drained soil.

GARDENING BY MONTH

LAGERSTROEMIA INDICA (CRAPE MYRTLE)

Known more as a familiar planting of the Southeast, this new hybridized form of Crape Myrtle (Lagerstroemia indica) can be successfully grown here in parts of the Northeast and Mid-Atlantic where the winters are harsher. These showy trees are a favorite of many due to their beautiful long-lasting blooms that appear near the end of July and last well into Fall, a bloom period of approximately 120 days! Three are numerous varieties of Crape Myrtle ranging in mature size and bloom color from the smaller shrub-like form to tree form, most cold hardy in zones 6-9, depending on the cultivar. Colors range from light to dark pink to purple, lavender, red and white. Through experience, I have found the 'Sioux', 'Catawba' and 'Natchez' cultivars to be most hardy. Crape Myrtle are deer resistant, butterfly and hummingbird friendly and drought tolerant once established. They grow best in full sun in a well-drained soil with a pH of 5.0-6.5. These trees require little to no pruning but can be pruned to maintain a more compact shape or to remove any dead branches that may result from a harsh winter. If you are going to prune, wait until late winter or early spring after the last frost. The plants are dormant in winter and any flowering occurs on new growth so pruning will encourage new flower producing branches. Remove any dead branches, suckers growing from the base or weak twiggy branches and allow strong leader branches to keep the framework of the tree.

Crape Myrtle can be planted as either a multi-trunk or singular-trunk form. An important note worth mentioning is that Crape Myrtle (Lagerstroemia) are among the last plants to push out their new growth so if they appear to be dead at the end of winter going into spring just give them some time to come into their glory. Since they are later to push out their leaves, they do benefit from an early spring feeding of a high phosphorus-lower nitrogen 5-10-5 formula to promote good foliar growth and an abundance of blooms in July-August. Crape Myrtles are not susceptible to insects or disease but as with any landscape planting, they should be monitored and properly maintained to keep them in good health.

GARDENING BY MONTH

GARDENING BY MONTH

Chapter 8: The August Garden

As the month of August brings increased heat and humidity to the northeast and mid-Atlantic, the garden continues to thrive. While Crape Myrtle, hydrangea, astilbe, echinacea and rudbeckia continue to bloom, newcomers including buddleia, sedum, Russian sage, solidago, and sedum make their debut.

August is a time for further revitalization of the summer garden. Perennials can be addressed at this time to extend their bloom season into the fall. Cut back browned foliage and stalks on perennials such as salvia and perform a full rejuvenation of daylilies. To perform this rejuvenation, completely remove any browned or yellowed foliage and seed stalks. This can be done using shears or manually while wearing gardening gloves. If plants need an extensive rejuvenation, there may be minimal remaining foliage, but in time, both newer lush green foliage and blooms will reappear. Also, daylilies, bearded iris, garden phlox, poppies, and peony can be dug and divided during August through September.

Continue to keep on top of weeds, before they go to seed and water trees deeply during lack of rain, as they are more vulnerable to drought. Reminder: a good layer of mulch or compost helps retain moisture around roots during the "dog days" of summer. Also, check regularly for signs of fungal or insect damage and treat, as they are more prominent during late summer. Continue to remove any dead, dying or diseased foliage and dispose of properly.

Mid-August to mid-October is prime lawn renovation and seeding time in the northeast and mid-Atlantic. It is also a good time to harvest vegetables, plan your fall crops and sow/collect seeds for fall or spring blooms. Butterflies and hummingbirds are frequent, should you plant the right flowers!

GARDENING BY MONTH

~AUGUST~

BUDDLEIA 'PUGSTER BLUE' (DWARF BUTTERFLY BUSH)

Hardy in USDA zones 5-9, Buddleia 'Pugster Blue' is a whole new variety of butterfly bush displaying the full-sized blooms normally seen on a standard plant, but on a compact 2-3 foot high by wide shrub. This newer cultivar has studier stems, large deeper purple blooms, and flowers a little later than Buddleia 'Blue Chip'. 'Pugster Blue' is an attraction to hummingbirds, butterflies, and Hummingbird Moths! It prefers a location with full sun with moderate watering, is drought tolerant once established and is deer resistant. As with other Buddleia, blooms develop on the new wood of the season. Pruning in late winter/early spring before new growth appears will help encourage a fuller plant with more blooms.

GARDENING BY MONTH

HYDRANGEA PANICULATA 'TARDIVA'

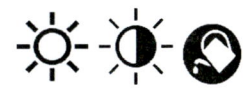

One of the latest blooming Hydrangea, Hydrangea 'Tardiva' will bring you right through fall with its fragrant white panicle blooms. Hardy in USDA zones 3-8, lacy white blooms fade to pink as the season progresses on a 6-10 foot tall by wide shrub or small tree. Plant this cultivar in full sun to partial shade with moderate watering and a well-drained soil. 'Tardiva' blooms on the new wood of the season. Prune in late winter/early spring to promote fullness and more abundant blooms.

SEDUM SPECTABILE 'BRILLIANT' (STONECROP)

☼ ⬤

Sedum is a hardy, low maintenance perennial available in a variety of sizes and colors. Sedum spectabile 'Brilliant', hardy in USDA zones 4-8, is a more compact border stonecrop, growing to a height and width of 12-18 inches. Huge clusters of mauve-pink blooms appear above light green succulent-like foliage in mid-summer and last into fall. Plant Sedum in full sun to part shade in a well-drained soil. Sedum is an attraction to pollinators and is drought resistant once established. This planting of Sedum is complemented by Ajuga 'Burgundy Glow', which blooms earlier in the season but continues to display its burgundy-purple foliage. Other varieties of compact sedum include Sedum 'Neon' and Sedum 'Pure Joy' (each hardy in USDA zones 3-9).

SEDUM SPECTABILE 'AUTUMN JOY' (STONECROP)

Another ever popular variety of Sedum is Sedum spectabile 'Autumn Joy', which is hardy in USDA zones 3-9. It displays voluminous pinkish-red blooms in late summer that are an attraction to pollinators. 'Autumn Joy' grows to a taller 18-24 inches high and prefers full sun to partial shade and a well-drained soil. In the backdrop of this planting is evergreen Blue Globe Montgomery Spruce, complementing the interesting foliage of sedum. Little to no maintenance is required for this perennial. Once the blooms fade, they continue to provide interest in the landscape throughout fall. In late autumn, remove any mushy stalks right to the ground. Light green rosette-like buds will be visible for next season's growth.

SEDUM INTERMEDIA 'LIME TWISTER' (STONECROP)

Among the groundcover varieties of sedum is Sedum intermedia 'Lime Twister'. Hardy in USDA zones 4-9, 'Lime Twister' is a newer cultivar with ground hugging two tone lime green succulent foliage edged with creamy-yellow highlights.

Soft pink flower clusters appear in late summer on a 4-inch tall by 18-inch-wide plant and last well into fall. Plant 'Lime Twister' in full sun to partial shade in a well-drained soil. This perennial is drought tolerant once established and is an attraction to pollinators. Other groundcover cultivars of sedum include, but are not limited to, Sedum spurium 'Dragon's Blood' (rose red blooms, 4-6 inches tall by 10-12 inches wide), Sedum rupestre 'Angelina' (yellow blooms, 3-6 inches tall by 24-36 inches wide), Sedum 'Lemon Ball' (chartreuse blooms, 4-6 inches tall by 10-12 inches wide) and Sedum spurium 'Fulda Glow' (rose red blooms, 4 inches tall by 10-12 inches wide). Each is hardy in USDA zones 3-9.

PEROVSKIA (RUSSIAN SAGE)

Russian Sage, hardy in USDA zones 4-9, is known for its long bloom season from late summer into late fall. Growing 3 to 4-feet tall by 2-3 feet wide, Perovskia produces clumps of upright greyish foliage that leads to spikes of violet-blue flowers. Plant

Russian Sage in full sun in a well-drained soil in an area where it has room to grow. This perennial has low water needs and is drought tolerant once established. Its fragrant foliage is an attraction for pollinators such as bees and hummingbirds and is also a deterrent for deer, making this perennial deer resistant.

EUPATORIUM (JOE PYE WEED)

Eupatorium (Joe Pye Weed or White Snakeroot) is native to North America, is hardy in USDA zones 4-9 and displays enormous umbrella-like heads of deep pink blooms from late summer and into fall. This smaller version of Joe Pye Weed is Eupatorium dubium 'Little Joe' or Dwarf Joe Pye Weed, which matures to a more compact height and width of 24-30 inches high by 18-24 inches wide. Joe Pye Weed prefers to be planted in an area of full sun to partial shade and requires moderate watering. The foliage of Eupatorium is known to be undesirable to deer, while its blooms are highly attractive to butterflies.

LIATRIS SPICATA (BLAZING STAR)

Liatris spicata, otherwise known as Purple Gayfeather or Blazing Star, is an herbaceous perennial native to North America and hardy in USDA zones 4-9. Narrow spikes of mauve-purple blooms appear in late summer and last into fall with deadheading. Clumps of tall upright stems bear flowers opening from the top down on a 30-36 inch tall by 12-18-inch-wide plant. Plant Liatris in a location with full sun and moderate watering. It is drought tolerant once established and is considered relatively deer resistant. Deadheading spent blooms will extend the flowering season further into fall. The blooms are an attraction to bees, butterflies, and hummingbirds.

SOLIDAGO SPHACELATA 'GOLDEN FLEECE' (AUTUMN GOLDENROD)

Among the best forms of goldenrod, Solidago sphacelata 'Golden Fleece' is a popular perennial in the late summer perennial border. Hardy in USDA zones 4-9, 'Golden Fleece' is a newer cultivar developed for its outstanding display of golden yellow blooms on a bushy, compact habit which is quite distinguishable from the roadside types. 'Golden Fleece' grows to a height and width of 18-24 inches high by wide and prefers a location with full sun to partial shade, moderate watering, and a well-drained soil. This cultivar produces blooms from summer into mid-fall. Solidago is drought tolerant once established, deer resistant and an attraction to birds and butterflies. This cultivar does not cause allergies, as the pollen is sticky and not windblown.

HELIANTHUS ANNUUS (COMMON SUNFLOWER)

Native to North America, Helianthus annuus, otherwise known as annual or common Sunflower, could not go by without mention. This popular cultivar is a member of a genus of over seventy annual and perennial plants in the daisy family. Planted as seed or purchased in container, voluminous golden or multi-colored golden, orange, and maroon blooms form in later summer into fall on 4-5-foot-tall stalks. A perennial form of sunflower, Helianthus salicifolius 'First Light', hardy in USDA zones 6-9, displays smaller golden-yellow blooms on a clumping feather-like foliage that is 4-5 foot tall by 1-2-foot-wide. Plant Helianthus in a location with full sun, moderate watering, and a well-drained soil. Helianthus is an attraction to pollinators, such as bees and butterflies, and the dried seed heads are a major food source for birds.

GARDENING BY MONTH

Chapter 9: The September Garden: Fall Interest

There is something special about the changing seasons in the garden. While some look at the end of summer as a time of decline in the landscape, I look at it as a time of autumn interest and reflection. September has become one of my favorite times in the garden as temperatures moderate, blue skies are frequent and humid days turn into less humid ones. There is a slight crispness as the cooler breezes rush in during the morning and evening hours and the landscape transitions.

By the end of July through September, blooms including Crape Myrtle, Butterfly Bush, panicle hydrangea and sedum continue to add interest as liriope, ornamental grasses, bee blossom and lobelia add to the ongoing view. Rejuvenated daylily and salvia continue to bloom into fall, as the bright red fruit on Dogwood and formation of berries on hollies become evident.

Now that the extreme heat of August has passed, September is an optimum time for planting. Cooler temperatures allow for better root development and less stress for plants. Ideally, planting should occur one to two months before the first frost date to allow adequate time for feeder roots to establish. As September progresses, continue to deadhead roses and perennials and remove broken branches off trees and shrubs to avoid future damage. Avoid pruning evergreens and deciduous trees and shrubs this month. Prune non spring-flowering deciduous trees and shrubs once dormant and evergreens during later winter to early spring. There is still time to divide and move perennials such as peony, lily, garden phlox, poppies, and bearded iris. Continue to harvest edibles and perform lawn renovation as needed.

GARDENING BY MONTH

~SEPTEMBER~

LIRIOPE MUSCARI 'VARIEGATA' (VARIEGATED LILYTURF)

Displaying blooms late summer into fall, Liriope 'Variegata' (Lilyturf) is a clump forming evergreen perennial, showing striped green and creamy white grass-like variegated foliage on an 8 to16 inch tall by 8-to12-inch-wide plant. Hardy in USDA zones 6-11, Liriope is perfect as a groundcover in areas of partial to full shade where ornamental grasses may have difficulty. In mid-summer to early fall, short spikes of deep purple flowers resembling tiny Grape Hyacinths appear, adding late season interest to the landscape. To promote new growth, remove any winter damaged foliage from this perennial in early spring once new foliage starts to emerge.

GARDENING BY MONTH

Another variety of Liriope, Liriope muscari 'Big Blue' displays deep green foliage and is hardy in USDA zones 5-11.

MISCANTHUS SINENSIS 'YAKU JIMA' (DWARF MAIDEN GRASS)

Hardy in USDA zones 5-9, Miscanthus sinensis 'Yaku Jima' is an outstanding dwarf maiden grass known for its pink plumes with tan overtones rising above the foliage in late summer into mid-fall. 'Yaku Jima' is comparable to Miscanthus 'Adiago', both growing to a height and width of 3-5 feet tall by wide. There are numerous forms of ornamental grasses ranging from dwarf fountain grasses, including Pennisetum alopecuroides 'Hameln' (USDA zones 4-9) growing to a mature size of 2-3 feet tall by wide, medium sized varieties including Pennisetum alopecuroides (USDA zones 5-9) growing 3-4 feet tall by wide and larger sized varieties including Calamagrostis acutiflora 'Karl Foerster' (USDA zones 4-9) reaching a mature size of 4-5 feet tall by 2-3 feet wide. Plant ornamental grasses in full sun to part shade in a well-drained soil. These hardy perennials are both deer resistant and drought tolerant once established.

DWARF MAIDEN GRASS 'YAKU JIMA' LATE SUMMER

DWARF MAIDEN GRASS 'YAKU JIMA' AUTUMN-WINTER

CARYOPTERIS CLANDONENSIS (BLUE MIST SHRUB)

Caryopteris clandonensis, commonly called Bluebeard, Blue Spirea, or Blue Mist, is a low-mounded, deciduous shrub that is valued for its aromatic foliage and late summer blooms that resemble clouds or a morning mist. This hybrid was discovered as an accidental cross between C. incana and C. mongholica. Caryopteris is hardy is USDA zones 5-8 and grows to a height and width of 2-3 feet. Plant this late summer flowering shrub in a well-drained soil and location with full sun. Blue Mist Shrub is drought tolerant once established, deer resistant, and an attraction for pollinators such as butterflies and hummingbirds.

HYPERICUM INODORUM 'MAGICAL UNIVERSE' (ST. JOHN'S WORT)

Hardy in USDA zones 5-8, and growing 2-3 feet high by wide, Hypercium, otherwise known as St. John's Wort, is a compact selection with dark green foliage and small, bright yellow, showy flowers that appear in June. The real highlight is the bright red fruit that forms later in summer, darkening to a deep red in fall, and contrasting against changing foliage. This cultivar is easy to grow with summer color from flowers and fruit until frost. Plant St. John's Wort in a location with full sun to partial shade and moderate watering. Prune back each spring to encourage new growth and flowering. This shrub is known to be deer resistant.

GAURA LINDHEIMERI (BEE BLOSSOM)

Hardy in USDA zones 6-9, Gaura is a heat and drought tolerant, deer resistant herbaceous perennial that grows to 15-48 inches tall by wide. Gaura lindheimeri prefers to be grown in full sun in a light to sandy soil with good drainage. Gaura produces delicate pink or white blooms from early summer that persist though mid-fall and is an attraction to butterflies. Excellent drainage is the key with this perennial, as it prefers a poor soil, making it thrive almost on neglect. Cut back stems after the first bloom to encourage re-blooming into fall.

LOBELIA CARDINALIS (CARDINAL FLOWER)

Lobelia is an herbaceous perennial and excellent addition to shady, wet locations. Hardy in USDA zones 4-9, Lobelia cardinalis forms upright stalks of scarlet red flowers in mid to late summer on a 24-inch tall by 18-24-inch-wide plant. Plant Lobelia in a location with partial to full shade and moderate watering. Blooms open from bottom to top and last into fall. Another variety of Lobelia is Lobelia siphilitica, or 'Great Blue' Cardinal Flower. This native species, hardy in USDA zones 4-9, produces heads of dark blue to white flowers throughout late summer and into fall on a 2-3 foot tall by 1-2-foot-wide plant. Lobelia is an attraction to hummingbirds and butterflies.

CHELONE LYONII 'HOT LIPS' (TURTLEHEAD)

Chelone lyonii, otherwise known as Turtlehead, is a moisture loving native wildflower, producing showy blooms late summer and into fall. Hardy in USDA zones 3-8, Chelone produces upright mounds of shiny green foliage followed by upright stems of large rosy-pink hooded blooms that resemble turtle heads poking out of their shell. This 24-30 inch tall by 18-24-inch-wide herbaceous perennial prefers a location with partial to full shade and a wet to moderately moist soil. It is an excellent addition to woodland and water gardens, bog areas and native plantings. New spring green foliage is tinted with a bronze hue. To encourage stronger stems and fullness, pinch foliage back in mid-spring when plants are about six inches tall. Chelone attracts butterflies and hummingbirds and the seed heads are enjoyed by birds.

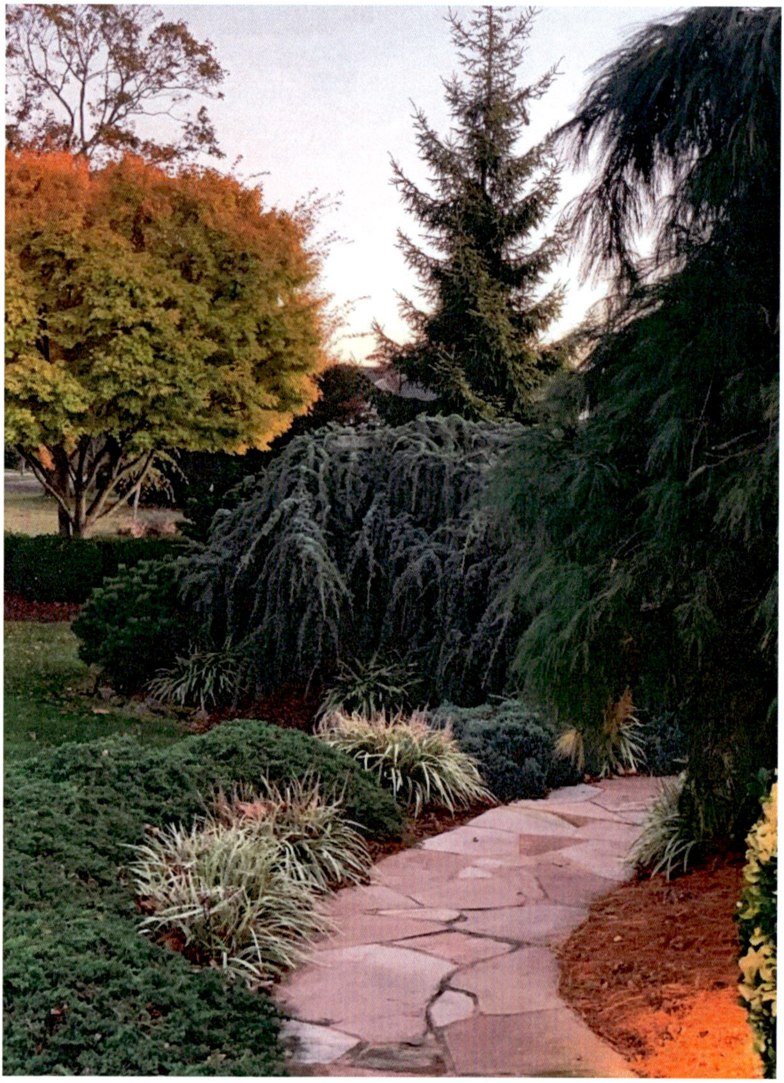

Chapter 10: The October Garden

As autumn is underway and the colors of the changing seasons start to become evident, daytime temperatures decline and there is a slight chill in the air. It is the time of year when temperatures are perfect for working in the garden and a few warm days are considered a heat wave. It is a time when the garden can be looked upon as either getting ready to go to sleep, or just preparing for the next big display. The plants prominent in the fall landscape can show interest either in blooms, berries or color of foliage and may provide blooms starting in summer that persist into the autumn months, adding continuing interest to the landscape.

To prepare your garden for fall, remove annuals that have completed flowering from containers or garden beds. To prevent fungal disease, clip back foliage on perennials which have finished their season. Two plants that come to mind are Hosta and peony. I remove the decaying foliage on Hosta to prevent fungal infection and to prevent slugs from laying their eggs in the dormant foliage. Peony stalks should be cut to the ground once the foliage is completely brown in mid to late October to eliminate risk of fungal infection. Lightly brush surrounding mulch between the cut stalks for additional protection.

It is recommended at this time to remove the browned stalks of perennials, such as salvia, and leave the lower green foliage until it is completely brown. Leaving the remaining green foliage will allow the perennial to continue photosynthesis and ensure the production of food to overwinter the plant. You may even experience a few more blooms into the fall season from making this part of your practice. Some flower seed heads such as those from echinacea and rudbeckia are a healthy food source for birds, so I leave those for the month of October, until all the seeds have either been eaten or have fallen from the plant. (Note: If there are any signs of diseased or damaged foliage, such as black leaf spot on your Rudbeckia, remove the foliage and dispose of it properly.)

The foliage of certain evergreen or semi-evergreen perennials such as heuchera, liriope, dianthus and ajuga should be left in autumn, and not cut back. They provide winter interest and can be prone to cold damage, so it is best to leave them until spring and remove only damaged foliage after the winter months. The same applies to ornamental grasses. Extreme cold without the insulation of snow can cause the centers of ornamental grasses to hollow out, so it is best to wait until spring to cut them back. Do not cut back foliage on evergreen sedges for it can damage the plant! If needed in spring, prune off only any winter damaged tips to improve the appearance. Decayed foliage (usually underneath the plant) can be removed anytime to prevent disease. With cooler autumn temperatures and more frequent rainfall, October can also be an optimum time for weeds. It is recommended to keep them in check by removing them now, before they become a nuisance later.

At the end of October and into November is the time to plant your spring flowering bulbs. Snowdrops, Crocus, Daffodils, Hyacinths, Tulips and Allium are a few selections that can bring interest to your spring garden. Here is a quick reference to planting depth for some common bulbs. Ideally, spring flowering bulbs should be planted when evening temperatures range between 40 to 50 degrees and at least six weeks before the ground freezes. (Note: In more northern areas, such as Maine, Vermont, and New Hampshire, you may need to adjust your planting time to somewhere between late September and mid-October). Dig to the proper depth, loosen the surrounding soil, and add a slow-release fertilizer such as bone meal to the soil underlying the bulb. Cover the bulb and add a thin layer of mulch for protection.

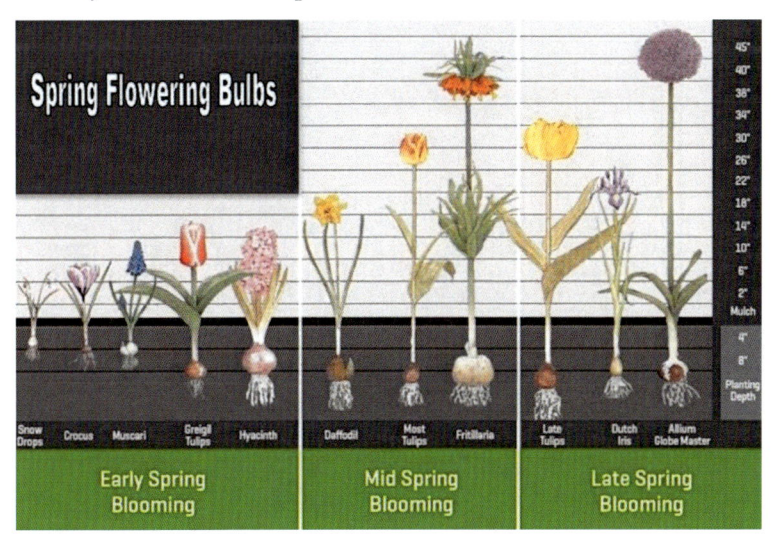

Dahlias are not winter hardy in colder climates. In zones 7 and under, once they are done blooming for the season, wait until after the first frost, then lift tuberous roots and store them during the colder months. Remove any remaining foliage while in the ground and carefully remove not to break the root. Once dug, gently shake off any remaining soil and pack the dry tuberous roots in a loose fluffy medium such as vermiculite. Store them over winter in a well-ventilated frost-free space, such as a garage, and start over in spring.

October is a busy month in the garden as far as garden chores are concerned and there can still be blooms and seasonal interest while the winter preparation is going on. Following are some plant recommendations to keep your gardening season going.

GARDENING BY MONTH

~OCTOBER~

CHRYSANTHEMUM MORIFOLIUM (HARDY GARDEN MUM)

Chrysanthemum morifolium, or hardy garden mum, is a classic addition to the fall garden. Hardy in USDA zones 5-9, Chrysanthemum produces slightly fragrant blooms in a large range of colors from white to pink, lavender, orange, yellow, bronze and multi-colored hybrids. Flowers can vary in appearance from single daisy-like blooms to double blooms. Chrysanthemum grows to a height and width of 1-2 feet tall by 2-3 feet wide and prefers a location with full sun to part shade and moderate watering. Blooms appear in late summer and last into fall, adding beautiful color to the autumn garden border.

To promote fullness, pinch back foliage in spring when plants are 6-8 inches tall.

SYMPHYOTRICHUM NOVAE-ANGLIAE (NEW ENGLAND ASTER)

Asters come in a variety of sizes and colors and bloom during late summer and into mid-fall. This variety, Aster 'Kickin Carmine Red', displays beautiful magenta blooms on a 24 to 36 inch-high by wide plant. Asters are native to North America, are easy to grow and make wonderful accents during the Fall season. Plant Aster in full sun in a moderately moist soil. Aster is hardy in a range of USDA zones from 5-9; however, hardiness can vary depending on each individual variety. Asters tend to be undesirable to deer, but rabbits enjoy them. If rabbits are chomping on your fall asters, leading to no blooms, place soap shavings around the plant. Our four-legged friends do not like the smell and will leave your plants alone!

NIPPONANTHEMUM NIPPONICUM (MONTAUK DAISY)

Nipponanthemum nipponicum (Montauk Daisy) is a favorite for the fall garden and produces blooms that last for weeks from October through frost. Native to the coastal regions of Japan, this perennial has been naturalized as a planting which can be seen along the New York, Long Island and New Jersey shorelines. A mature specimen of this plant will reach a height and width of approximately 1.5-3 feet while displaying two to three-inch white flower heads with bright yellow centers on a shrub-like plant. The plant's foliage is toothed and slightly leather-like. Hardy in USDA zones 5-9, Montauk Daisy (also known as Nippon Daisy) prefers to be grown in full sun in a well-drained soil. Do not allow the plant to sit in water as this perennial will not tolerate too much moisture around its roots. To keep compact and upright, prune back new growth of the actively growing plant to half its height in late spring to early summer. In areas where the woody stems do not die back in winter, prune back the stems and foliage at the end of the growing season. This species is relatively disease resistant, salt and drought tolerant, pollinator friendly, and undesirable to rabbit and deer.

CALLICARPA AMERICANA (AMERICAN BEAUTYBERRY)

Callicarpa americana (American Beautyberry) is a native North American deciduous shrub that is known for its long arching branches and clusters of glossy iridescent purple berries that are produced in autumn. Hardy in USDA zones 6-10, Beautyberry grows to a height and width of approximately 3 to 6 feet and prefers a location with full sun to partial shade and moderate watering. The shrub will tolerate a range of soil types but prefers a moist clay or sandy soil with organic matter.

The fruit of Beautyberry is non-toxic to humans and animals and is an important food source for many species of birds, mainly the Northern Bobwhite, and insignificant flowers are a nectar source for pollinators. The foliage of Callicarpa is a favorite of White-tailed deer. American Beautyberry blooms on the new wood of the season and usually does not require much maintenance. If desired, the shrub can be pruned to rejuvenate or control its size in late winter or early spring. The berries remain on the plant for up to six weeks or longer after the shrub drops its leaves and are known for their use in making a delicious jelly. American Beautyberry serves nicely in areas such as woodland borders and does well as an understory planting. Besides the American Beautyberry (Callicarpa americana), other species of beautyberry include Bodinier's Beautyberry (Callicarpa bodinieri), Japanese Beautyberry (Callicarpa japonica) and Chinese Beautyberry (Callicarpa dichotoma), each cold hardy to USDA zone 5. Above is Callicarpa americana in full view. Notice the long arching branches and changing foliage that turns from deep green to a lime green hue as the fruit of Callicarpa becomes vibrant. This is certainly one of this gardener's favorites for autumn interest in the landscape!

VIBURNUM DILATATUM 'CARDINAL CANDY'

Hardy in USDA zones 4-8, Viburnum dilatatum 'Cardinal Candy' is a deciduous, cold hardy shrub bearing creamy white blooms followed by large bright red berries that persist through winter. This variety of viburnum displays an upright habit, reaching a height and width of 5 feet, and prefers a location with full sun to partial shade and a loamy to normal soil. The berries are bird friendly and wildlife will feast on this shrub for months. Viburnum dilatatum 'Cardinal Candy' is also known to be deer resistant. For best fruiting, group two or more plants together.

TRICYRTIS HIRTA (TOAD LILY)

Tricyrtis hirta (Toad Lily), hardy in USDA zones 4-9, is a shade loving perennial that bears dainty orchid-like blooms on 2 to 3-foot-tall stalks in autumn. Toad Lily is practically maintenance free if planted in the correct location. It performs best in deep shade with a moist soil and sheltered from windy conditions. Feed Toad Lily with a slow-release organic fertilizer to keep it at its best. In more northern locations,

Tricyrtis hirta may bloom late summer into fall if located in an area with a little more sunlight.

ANEMONE HUPEHENSIS (JAPANESE ANEMONE)

Hardy in USDA zones 4-8, Japanese Anemone is a perennial available in a multitude of colors including snow white, light to dark pink to purple and is known for having one of the longest bloom seasons. Japanese Anemone is herbaceous, possesses a clumping habit, and spreads by rhizomes once established, making it suitable for cottage gardens, coastal areas, and naturalized areas such as prairies and meadows. Plant Japanese Anemone in full sun to partial shade in a location with a moist, yet well-drained soil. This perennial grows to a height and width of 2 to 4 feet, so give it plenty of room to mature. Anemone is low maintenance once established and is known to be both deer and rabbit resistant. It is also salt tolerant and an attraction for butterflies. Flowers start in summer and last up to six to eight weeks well into fall, bringing interest to the garden and extending the gardening season.

LONICERA SEMPERVIRENS (TRUMPET HONEYSUCKLE)

Hardy in USDA zones 4-9, Lonicera sempervirens, or Trumpet Honeysuckle, is a vigorous climbing vine showing long tubular red blooms with yellow interiors that are an attraction to butterflies, bees, hummingbirds, and some moth pollinators. Small red berries produced in late summer to early fall are a food source for birds and foliage is an attraction to white tailed deer. This plant is non-invasive like some other species of honeysuckle and is most suitable in vertical spaces as on a trellis, or as an addition to butterfly and pollinator gardens. Trumpet Honeysuckle grows to a mature height and width of 10-20 feet high by 3-6 feet wide and grows best in full sun with moderate watering and a well-drained soil. Foliage is mostly deciduous in more northern areas and semi-evergreen in zones 6-7. Flowers begin in late spring to early summer, and peak interest takes place in fall as the blooms continue to show!

DAHLIA PINNATA (DAHLIA)

When one thinks of autumn, Dahlia often come to mind. Petite to dinner plate size blooms in a multitude of colors, appear in mid-summer and last well into fall as other blooms are fading. Plants mature to 1-5 foot tall by 1-2-foot-wide and prefer a location with full sun, moderate watering, and a rich well-drained, slightly acidic soil. Dahlia are planted as tubers in spring after the last frost date and dug up to be stored for winter. They are perennials in warmer climates and considered annuals in our region but could not go without mention! I have seen blooms lasting well into the end of October during milder seasons. Dahlias are an attraction to butterflies and hummingbirds and make beautiful cut flowers.

GARDENING BY MONTH

GARDENING BY MONTH

Chapter 11: The November-December Garden: Winter Has Arrived

As the garden slowly goes to rest, and nature displays all its colorful beauty, there is still much to be done. For starters, autumn and early winter are the perfect time to continue eliminating those annoying weeds. It can be a battle with clover and baby maple trees attempting to take over tightly grown perennials such as coreopsis all summer, but as the perennials go dormant, invaders are easier to spot and remove. Don't get me wrong. I am a fan of clover for it is pollinator friendly, but I prefer when it behaves itself and doesn't grow in an unwanted spot! November is also a good time for continued bulb planting. Depending on your zone, this task may already be completed or it is on the schedule for the near future.

Pruning is a discussion that often comes up around this time of year. I often get the question, "Do I prune now or in the spring?" Generally speaking, prune flowering trees and shrubs immediately after flowering in spring or summer. There are some exceptions such as spirea, and buddleia, as discussed in earlier chapters. Pruning of evergreens is not recommended in the fall, as it can spark new growth that may be unable to harden off before the first frost. For deciduous non-flowering trees and shrubs, if the temperatures are dropping into the 40's at night, wait until the plant becomes dormant. At that point you can shape the tree or shrub without harm. Broken or damaged branches can be eliminated anytime.

Fall is also a good time for moving deciduous trees and shrubs such as Weeping Japanese Maple, while they are dormant. For a safe transition, prune the roots around the root ball approximately 8-12 inches deep with a sharp spade three to six months prior to transplanting. This promotes the tree to develop new feeder roots, allowing greater access to nutrients. Give the plant a good watering to hydrate it one or two days before moving. Be sure to get a good rootball when digging and place the rootball in burlap for moving to keep the roots intact. Dig the hole in the new location before moving, position the root flare slightly above the grade and backfill with a good organic enriched topsoil. Mulch around the plant to help retain moisture and water in thourghly. Keep the plant well hydrated as it adjusts to its new location.

A common practice among homeowners is the removal of fallen leaves. We have been taught over the years that leaves can suffocate a lawn and should not be left. This is true only if more than 10-20% of your lawn is covered with a thick layer of leaf matter, which can be an invitation to mold disease and critters, smother grass and inhibit new growth in spring. On the other hand, a light layer of shredded leaves can add nutrients to your lawn and will feed a vast number of microbes which are beneficial for soil health. Adding shredded leaves to your garden beds serves as a mulch and insulator, prevents soil loss and provides nutrients. Fallen leaves are also a source of food, shelter and nesting material for wildlife, and can provide protection for pollinators, including wooly bear caterpillars, great spangled fritiaries, luna moths and ground bees.

Should you be looking for a tidier look to your lawn, autumn leaves can also be a beneficial addition to the home compost pile or left in a pile alone to decay. By springtime the lower portion of the pile will have been converted into a nutrient rich soil, while the middle and top layers can be used as mulch.

Once autumn has passed and winter is underway, snow may be in the forecast. While snow is a good insulator, a helpful tip is to prune any over-weighted branches from trees in autumn to prevent breakage. Some multi-leader evergreens such as Emerald Green Arborvitae can be prone to snow damage from overweighted branches. Before the snow arrives, arbor tie any loose or dangling branches to the main trunk or other sturdy branch to prevent damage. After the snow, it may be tempting to remove pile up from weighted branches; however, this is a good time to exercise caution. Beneath the snow could also be a frozen layer of ice. Any manipulating of the frozen branches could result in easy breakage and permanent damage to your plant. To remove excess weight, carefully dig around the trapped branches to loosen the snow and allow them to spring back up on their own. Never shake branches with ice. It is best to let nature take its course and allow thawing to occur. The branches will gradually regain their shape as the ice melts preventing any harm to your landscaping.

As the seasons change, with possible snow covering the garden, there can still be interest in the landscape. Here are some landscape plants to enhance your November-December garden. Some can be noticed for their berries, some for their foliage and even some for their blooms during a time when other plants are dormant.

GARDENING BY MONTH

~NOVEMBER-DECEMBER~

ILEX VERTICILLATA (WINTERBERRY)

Ilex verticillata or Winterberry, a native to the swampy areas of northeastern North America, is a deciduous holly known for its display of bright red berries that appear on bare branches in winter. Hardy in USDA zones 4-8, Winterberry grows to a height and width between 3-12 feet tall by wide and prefers to be grown in full sun to partial shade in a moderately moist soil. Winterberries are dioecious, meaning they need a male and female to produce fruit. The female shrub requires a pollinator such as Jim Dandy for the berries to set. Berries are very showy, persist through winter, and are a feast for wintering birds and small mammals. This shrub is an excellent addition for moist, low lying locations such as near streams or ponds and serves well in native, rain and bird friendly gardens. Winterberry is not edible by humans and pets.

ILEX MESERVEAE 'GOLDEN GIRL' (GOLD FRUITED BLUE HOLLY)

Hardy in USDA zones 5-9, Ilex meserveae 'Golden Girl' is a dense multi-stemmed evergreen known for its dark olive-green leaves and unusual yellow berries that appear in fall and last through winter. Developed by horticulturist Kathleen Meserve from Long Island, and introduced into the market in 1989, this hybrid is a cross between the yellow fruited English holly, Ilex aquifolium 'Fructa Lutea' and Ilex rugosa. Golden Girl Holly produces insignificant flowers that turn into fruit on the new wood of the season and grows to a mature height and width of 12 feet tall by 8 feet wide. It prefers a location with full to partial sun and a moist, but well-drained soil. To produce berries, this female holly requires a male pollinator such as Ilex'

Blue Prince', 'Blue Boy' or 'Blue Stallion'. The fruit of Golden Girl Holly is an attraction to birds.

ILEX VERTICILLATA 'AFTERGLOW' (WINTERBERRY)

This variety of winterberry, Ilex verticillata 'Afterglow', is a deciduous eye-catching landscape shrub admired for its outstanding vibrant orange-red fruit which appears in fall. Hardy in USDA zones 4-8, this cultivar reaches a height and width of six to eight feet and prefers a location with full to partial sun and a moist soil. It is a compact selection that stays smaller than most other winterberry cultivars. 'Afterglow' is a female plant and needs a male pollinator such as 'Jim Dandy' to produce fruit. One foliage drops, fruits remain on the plant through winter. 'Afterglow' winterberry is a North American native selection, tolerates road salt and urban pollution and is pollinator and bird friendly. Another variety of winterberry with orange berries is 'Little Goblin', growing to a mature height and width of 3-4 feet and hardy in USDA zones 3-9.

DAPHNE TRANSATLANTICA BLAFRA (ETERNAL FRAGRANCE DAPHNE)

Daphne, hardy in USDA zones 6-9, is a re-blooming evergreen shrub known for its profusion of showy blooms starting in late spring, but really steals the show throughout the autumn months for its continuation of fragrant light pink flowers through winter. Daphne is a slow growing, compact shrub, reaching a height and width of 24 to 30 inches tall by wide and prefers a location with partial to full sun and moderately moist soil. (Note: Daphne is evergreen in temperatures above 0 degrees Fahrenheit and ingestion of its bark and leaves can be hazardorus to pets). This colorful shrub is an attraction to butterflies and is undesirable to deer. Flowers bloom on old wood from the previous season.

CROCUS SPECIOSUS 'OXONIAN' (AUTUMN CROCUS)

While Crocus vernus is a welcomed sign of spring, Crocus speciosus, otherwise known as Autumn Crocus, is a welcomed sight in fall. Autumn Crocus 'Oxonian' is hardy in USDA zones 4-9, producing lilac stripped blooms with yellow centers on a six-inch-high plant in November, that last well into winter. Plant autumn crocus corms in early autumn in a location with full sun and a moderately moist well-drained soil. Autumn crocus is perfect for naturalized areas, as the corms multiply by offsets to create a mass planting.

CYCLAMEN HEDERIFOLIUM (HARDY CYCLAMEN)

Cyclamen hederifolium, or hardy Cyclamen, is a tuberous cold tolerant perennial which is perfect for mass plantings, naturalizing woodland areas and rock gardens. Hardy Cyclamen prefers a location with partial to full shade and a well-drained, rich organic soil. Hardy in USDA zones 5-9, this low growing perennial reaches a height and width of just 4 to 6 inches tall by 10 to 12 inches wide. Delicate rosy-pink, lavender, or white blooms appear first, followed by a backdrop of evergreen heart-shaped foliage early fall into early winter. The name cyclamen comes from the Latin term "cyclamnos", which means cycle, circle, or wheel, which refers to the wheel-like shape of the tubers. Cyclamen tubers can be planted in late summer into early fall, approximately one inch below the soil surface. Foliage lasts until spring and plants go completely dormant during the summer months. Hardy Cyclamen is known to be deer resistant.

ABELIA GRANDIFLORA 'KALEIDOSCOPE'

Hardy in USDA zones 6-9, Abelia grandiflora 'Kaleidoscope' is a deer resistant, drought tolerant, dwarf semi-evergreen shrub with changing foliage and a display of tubular fragrant pinkish-white blooms that appear in spring and continue into fall. 'Kaleidoscope' grows to a height and width of 2-3 feet tall by 3-4 feet wide and prefers a location of full to partial sun and a moist, but well-drained soil. The late season display continues as yellow-lime green foliage turns to a fiery orangey-red in autumn, bringing outstanding color to the fall landscape. Abelia 'Kaleidoscope' is one of the longest blooming Abelias and blooms on the new wood of the season, so pruning should be performed during late winter into early spring. Abelia is deer resistant and the blooms are an attraction to butterflies!

MAHONIA AQUIFOLIUM (OREGON GRAPE HOLLY) PHOTO CREDIT: WIKIMEDIA APRIL 2017 NINO BARBIERI

Hardy in USDA zones 6-9, Mahonia (Oregon Grape Holly) is a broad-leaved evergreen shrub with glossy leathery leaves, growing to a height and width of 3-6 feet tall by wide. Fragrant yellow flowers appearing in spring give way to golden berries that turn to blue-black by fall and are enjoyed by wildlife. The cluster of tiny grape-like fruits are edible with a bit of tartness and are often used to make delicious jams, jellies and preserves. Foliage emerges a reddish hue in spring, turning to dark green in summer, while continuing the show in winter by turning to a dark burgundy. Mahonia prefers an area with partial shade and a moderately moist, but well-drained soil. While this plant gives interest in just about every season, it shines during the late fall and winter months. Oregon Grape Holly is also deer resistant. Other hardy cultivars of Mahonia include Mahonia japonica (Japanese Mahonia) and Mahonia media (hybrid Mahonia).

MAHONIA AQUIFOLIUM FRUIT (PHOTO CREDIT: THOMON WIKIMEDIA COMMONS)

Just for fun! OREGON GRAPE JELLY: To make a delicious jelly from the fruit of Oregon Grape Holly, lightly crush three to five pounds of washed fruit by hand or with a blender on lowest speed, add three cups of water, and simmer the mixture for ten minutes while mashing slightly to release the juice. Pour the mixture into a colander covered in cheesecloth and allow it to drain until you have four cups of collected juice. Discard the pulp and stems and mix the gathered juice with five cups of sugar and bring to a full boil. You can also add a little lemon juice (¼ cup) for additional flavor. Add one package of liquid pectin and bring back to a full boil for one minute until the mixture reaches the jelly stage. The jelly will form a sheet as it leaves the spoon once it has reached the correct temperature. Pour the mixture into sterilized mason jars, cover, and allow to cool. Depending on taste, the recipe can be altered by adding additional fruit, a stick of cinnamon or perhaps liquor to sweeten the jelly. You can get as creative as you like!

MAHONIA MEDIA 'MARVEL' (HYBRID MAHONIA) BLOOM

Hardy in USDA zones 6-9, this hybrid form of Mahonia, Mahonia Media 'Marvel' puts on a show from late November into December, displaying sprays of fragrant bright yellow blooms on a 6-foot high by 4-foot-wide plant. Flowers are followed by grape like clusters of blue-black berries. This beauty really lights up the winter landscape!

GARDENING BY MONTH

ILEX 'NELLIE STEVENS' NOVEMBER BERRIES

ILEX 'NELLIE STEVENS' DECEMBER BERRIES

Ilex Nellie Stevens is a member of the Ilex genus, comprising of 400 to 600 varieties of trees and shrubs. It was named after Nellie R. Stevens of Oxford Maryland, who discovered this selection in the mid-1900's from a cross between Chinese Holly (Ilex cornuta) and English Holly (Ilex aquifolium). Hardy in USDA zones 6-9, 'Nellie Stevens' is a vigorous growing pyramidal shaped evergreen displaying glossy leathery dark green foliage with inconspicuous greenish-white blooms in spring followed by large bright red berries in fall. This popular cultivar grows to a height and width of 15 to 20 feet tall by 8 to 12 feet wide and does not require a male pollinator to fruit. Plant 'Nellie Stevens' Holly in full sun to partial shade in a moist, yet well-drained soil and allow it plenty of room to reach its full potential. Nellie Stevens Holly is capable of surviving drought-like conditions in winter and does not like having its "feet wet" from standing in poorly drained soil. Pruning of this tree is not necessary, but if shaping is desired, prune in spring once the threat of frost is gone. It is recommended to spray this broad-leaved evergreen with an anti-desiccant in fall to prevent winter drying from harsh winds. This tree serves nicely in an evergreen border or privacy screening. An additional attribute is that the berries are enjoyed by wintering birds.

CORNUS SANGUINEA 'COMPRESSA' (DWARF BLOODSTEM DOGWOOD)

Cornus sanguinea 'Compressa', or Dwarf Bloodstem Dogwood, is hardy in USDA zones 4-8, and widely admired for its interesting deep green multi-veined curly foliage that changes in color as the season progresses. Cornus sanguinea 'Compressa' displays a narrow columnar stature, reaching 6-8 feet high by 1-3 feet in width. In autumn, green foliage turns to a burgundy red, followed by bright burgundy-red stems in winter when the shrub is bare. Plant Dwarf Bloodstem Dogwood in a location with full sun to partial shade and moderate watering and enjoy its display during the winter months. Other dwarf dogwood varieties with bright red stems in winter include Cornus alba 'Elegantissima' (Variegated Red Twig Dogwood, hardy in USDA zones 2-8 and growing to 6-8 feet tall) and Cornus stolonifera (Red Fire Dogwood, hardy in USDA zones 2-7 and growing to 3-6 feet tall). Red Twig Dogwood are seldom touched by deer and are drought tolerant once established.

BETULA POPULIFOLIA 'WHITESPIRE'

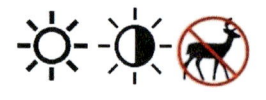

Betula populifolia 'Whitespire', hardy in USDA zones 3-7, is known for its attractive upright trunk with horizontal branches and beautiful non-exfoliating white bark streaked with gray markings, which is most striking during the winter months when the tree is bare. Betula 'Whitespire' grows to a mature size of 20-40 feet tall by 10-20 feet wide and prefers a location with full sun to part shade and a moderately moist soil. Long serrated green leaves appear in spring and turn yellow at the end of the season adding interest to the autumn garden. This variety is more heat tolerant and resistant to both disease and bronze birch borer when compared to other white-barked trees. Other members of Betula family exhibiting beautiful exfoliating bark include Betula jacquemontii (Himalayan Birch), Betula papyrifera (Paper Birch) and Betula nigra (River Birch). Trees in this family are known to be deer resistant.

ACER PALMATUM 'SANGO KAKU' (CORAL BARK MAPLE)

Acer palmatum 'Sango Kaku', otherwise known as Coral Bark Maple, is a deciduous tree known for its showy pinkish red (coral-colored) bark that glows in the winter landscape. Hardy in USDA zones 5-8, Coral Bark Maple displays yellow-green leaves with reddish margins in spring that mature to light green by summer and turn yellow-gold in fall. After the foliage drops in autumn, red coloration appears on younger twigs, which becomes more pronounced with colder temperatures or after a snowfall. 'Sango Kaku' requires minimal maintenance and stays relatively compact, growing to a mature size of 20-25 feet tall by 15-20 feet wide. Plant in full sun to partial shade with moderate watering and try to avoid locations with high winds for best results.

Coral Bark Maple may go dormant in winter, but it is the bark which is the highlight during the colder months. Seen here are the vibrant stems of 'Sango Kaku' in the landscape once its autumn foliage falls, extending interest as the rest of the garden sleeps.

Now that we have covered a selection of cultivars for creating the all-season landscape, the following chapter will provide some helpful maintenance tips to keep your garden at its best.

Chapter 12: Plant Maintenance Tips

WATERING: When establishing new plants, water thoroughly after planting and keep your garden well-watered throughout the first growing season until plant root systems are established. Feel down by the roots or use a moisture meter to determine whether the plant is getting the correct moisture. The soil surrounding the root-ball should appear moist but not wet or overly dry. Remember clay type soils tend to hold more moisture, whereas sandy soils drain more rapidly, so alter your watering accordingly. Do not rely on rainfall or lawn sprinklers alone as they may not supply an adequate amount of moisture. Watering new plantings by hand, two or three times a week to supplement your irrigation system is recommended in extreme summer heat. When planting in fall, make sure your plantings get enough water until the ground freezes in winter and then when the ground thaws. If you do not have an irrigation system, the use of soaker hoses is recommended. Water should be applied at a rate of 3/4 inch of water every three days or 1-1 ½ inches a week. (One inch of water goes down 6 " into the soil.)

MONITORING YOUR PLANTS: Improper watering is one of the major causes leading to the demise of plantings. One of the first signs of a plant in stress is often seen in changes in the coloring of the foliage. Generally, yellowing leaves indicate too much moisture, while browning leaves indicate dryness and lack of water. Healthy roots should appear light in color (white or tan) while unhealthy roots appear brown or black and indicate possible root rot, caused by too much moisture and insufficient oxygen. Use a moisture meter to determine the wetness or dryness of the soil and adjust your watering accordingly.

INSECT AND DISEASE CONTROL: Periodically check your plants for insect or fungal damage and treat if needed. While there are numerous insects and diseases that can cause damage to plantings, there are two cases I come across regularly as a landscape designer. A common fungal disease that often attacks certain broad-leaved evergreens such as Skip and Cherry Laurel is Shot Hole Fungus. This disease occurs mostly during times of high humidity and frequent rainfall and is signified by circular holes and brown spots on the foliage of the plant. Common on Euonymus is a condition known as Powdery Mildew. Powdery Mildew can be recognized by the appearance of tiny flecks of white on the foliage and stems that comes off as a powder when shaken. If you see either one of these conditions, spray with a systemic fungicide and apply monthly to keep the condition in check. (Note: While foliar sprays are absorbed through only the leaves, systemic applications go directly to the entire plant and are generally more effective.)

Other plantings such as roses, hydrangea and rhododendron are also susceptible to fungal attack and should be treated in the same manner. Fungal infections that attack roses are often caused by constant moisture on the foliage, which can be controlled by drip irrigation rather than watering from above. Another common condition is scale, in which insects feed off the trunk or stems of the plant, resulting in dieback of branches and loss of foliage. If you notice scale, rub the circular white patch with your finger. After rubbing the patch of white, if there is an underlying orange color, the insect is alive, and treatment is recommended. While fungal infections should be addressed with a systemic fungicide, Scale is best treated with an insecticidal spray. Practicing a regular insect and fungal control maintenance program will keep your plants healthy.

EVERGREENS: Most evergreens can be pruned at any time of year except when the weather is too hot or right before temperatures start to drop below freezing. Ideally the best time is believed to be in March before new growth starts. This also eliminates any winter burn that can occur during especially cold weather and gives the evergreen a good start for spring. Most evergreens will not take well to hard pruning. The only exception is Taxus (Yew) which may rejuvenate over time. No plant is completely maintenance free so keep your evergreens trimmed to their desired size. This will also keep them full and healthy and prevent thinning out. NOTE: Evergreens will shed their inner needles or foliage in the Fall/Spring to allow for new growth. If any branches appear brown or dead after planting or after winter, trim them off and allow the plant to rejuvenate. When in doubt ask a professional.

WINTER CARE: BROAD LEAVED EVERGREENS: Some broad-leaved evergreens such as Cherry, Skip, or Mountain Laurel, Japanese Aucuba, Leucothoe, Rhododendron, Holly, Boxwood or Euonymus can be subject to winter burn from dehydration caused by water loss in the case of a cold and dry winter. Care should be taken in the usage of an anti-desiccant spray which should be applied around Thanksgiving time (when daytime temperatures are in the 50's and evening temperatures in the 40's) and again if there is a thaw during the winter months. Only apply when the temperatures are above freezing and no rain in the forecast for 24 hours. NEVER allow anti-desiccant to get onto the foliage of Hinoki Cypress, for it can be detrimental to the plant.

GARDENING BY MONTH

FLOWERING SHRUBS: Generally, flowering deciduous shrubs and evergreens should be pruned after the bloom (late August into fall) Flowering shrubs such as some varieties of hydrangea bloom on the last year's growth and will not bloom if cut back in spring. Shrubs such as Spirea and Buddleia improve bloom when cut back in late winter/early spring (March-April) once any threat of frost is gone and before developing new foliage. Renovate Lilac in winter and prune for shape after flowering in spring. Prune roses in early spring to remove winter damage before new growth starts.

ROSES: Apply an all-in-one systemic food and insect/fungal control (such as Bayer All in One Rose & Flower Care) into the soil around each plant in early spring and once a month during the growing season to keep your roses looking beautiful. It is recommended to follow the dosage instructions located on the label. Deadheading of Knock Out Roses is not essential but doing so will keep your plants full.

TREES: Often hardwood trees, such as Crape Myrtle and Magnolia, will sprout vertical branches from the base or roots called "suckers" or "water sprouts", that can interfere with tree health. It is best to remove them before they cause damage. Prune (or move) deciduous trees in fall after leaves have fallen and tree is dormant. Evergreens can be moved in either spring or fall and must be keep well-watered.

GRASSES: Grasses should be cut back in late March before new growth appears. Leaving the grass during the winter provides interest to the garden and protects from winter damage.

PERENNIALS: Deadhead perennials such as salvia, daylily, and dianthus throughout summer for continuous repeat blooms. In fall, perennials should be allowed to die back, then remove any unwanted foliage. Pruning back perennials can be done in either late fall or early spring (March) before new growth appears but it is recommended in the Fall to prevent disease. Note: There are some perennials such as liriope (Lilyturf) and coral bells (Heuchera) that provide winter interest and should be pruned back in spring. Cut back Liriope in early spring (March/April) 2-2 ½ inches above the ground to allow for new growth. Remove winter damaged foliage from Coral Bells in early April. Do not cut back sedges. If golden Japanese Sedge has winter damage to its foliage after a harsh winter, run your fingers through the plant to remove any damaged fronds to allow for new growth. Wear gardening gloves to perform this procedure since the foliage can be sharp. This should be done in April or May.

FERTILIZING: Feed plants in spring and late summer. Do not apply a full dose if feeding in the fall. Apply a half dose for root feeding only. For new plantings, allow the plantings to become established then apply a slow-release organic fertilizer, or apply a "starter" formula when planting. For established plants there are several products on the market. Be careful not to buy a concentrated product that will burn the roots. A slow release or organic fertilizer such as Holly-tone is recommended. Once again, when in doubt ask a professional.

LAWN CARE: Ideally sod lawns are best planted in spring and seed best planted in the fall. For proper root development and germination, water newly planted sod and seed lawns twice daily for approximately 15 minutes until germination occurs, preferably in mid-morning and mid-afternoon (4-6 hours apart) to keep the soil moist but not wet. A newly planted seed lawn usually takes about two to three weeks to show growth.

For more established lawns, maintenance such as dethatching, core aeration and over-seeding are best done in the fall (best between August 15th and October 15th) to help rejuvenate the lawn and give it a healthy start for the following season. Dethatching involves the removal of dead grass and core aeration uses a machine to pull plugs from the lawn; hence, aerating the soil. Over-seeding is just as it sounds. New topsoil is applied with a layer of seed and starter fertilizer to give your lawn a makeover. Most varieties of grass thrive best with a soil pH between 5.8 and 7.2, which allows nutrients such as nitrogen to do their job. If low soil pH starts to inhibit the ability of your lawn to take up nutrients, signs are excess weeds, lawn moss and loss of vitality. Have your soil tested, and if needed, an application of lime, which will raise the pH, is best between fall and early spring. It is recommended to have a regular maintenance program to keep your lawn at its best.

Plants are living things and they require care, just as people do, to remain healthy and looking their best. Following these simple maintenance tips can become easy practice, allowing you to enjoy your accomplishments for many years to come. A garden can bring happiness and well-being to all those who encounter it. Simply choose one or more plants of interest per month that are to your liking, and you too can have something to look forward to every month of the year!

GARDENING BY MONTH

"Gardening is the art that uses flowers and plants as paint, and the soil and sky as canvas." ~ Elizabeth Murray

Index:

Abelia grandiflora
  'Kaleidoscope', 165
Acer palmatum 'Sango Kaku'
  Coral Bark Maple, 173
acidic soil, 15
Agastache
  Hyssop-Hummingbird Mint, 108
Agricultural lime, 16
Ajuga
  Bugleweed, 67
alkaline soils, 15
Allium 'Globemaster', 59
  Ornamental Onion, 59
Allium 'Mont Blanc'
  Ornamental Onion, 60
Aluminum sulfate, 16
annuals, 141
Asiatic Lilly
  Hybrid Garden Lily, 87
Aster 'Kickin Carmine Red'
  New England Aster, 145
Astilbe 'Sprite', 110
Astilbe 'Vision in Red', 90
Azalea, 56
Betula populifolia 'Whitespire', 172
Birch, 173
broad-leaved evergreens, 177
Buddleia 'Pugster Blue'
  Dwarf Butterfly Bush, 120
Buddleia davidii Low & Behold
  Dwarf Butterfly Bush, 113
butterflies, 61, 107, 127, 135, 137, 151, 152, 163, 166
Calamagrostis acutiflora 'Karl Foerster', 134
Callicarpa americana
  American Beautyberry, 147
Caryopteris
  Blue Mist Shrub, 135
Cercis canadensis
  Eastern Redbud, 54
Chaenomeles speciosa
  Flowering Quince, 35
Chelone lyonii
  Turtlehead, 139
Chrysanthemum morifolium
  Hardy Garden Mum, 144
Clematis, 93
Convallaria majalis
  Lily of the Valley, 44
Coreopsis 'Sunkiss'
  Tickseed, 83
Coreopsis verticillate 'Zagreb'
  Tickseed, 82
Creeping Phlox, 46
Crocus speciosus Autumn Crocus, 163
Crocus vernus
  Spring Crocus, 29
Cyclamen hederifolium
  Hardy Cyclamen, 164
Dahlia, 153
Daphne, 162

GARDENING BY MONTH

deer resistant, 22, 28, 32, 33, 34, 49, 59, 61, 68, 77, 82, 83, 85, 86, 91, 95, 100, 101, 107, 109, 110, 113, 117, 126, 127, 128, 135, 137, 150, 165, 167, 172, 173
Dethatching, 180
Dianthus
    Garden Pinks, 69
Dicenta spectabilis
    Bleeding Heart, 68
Digitalis purpurea
    Common Foxglove, 95
drought tolerant, 61, 83, 84, 91, 94, 108, 113, 117, 126, 127, 128, 137, 147, 165, 172
Dwarf Bloodstem Dogwood, 171
dwarf maiden grass, 133
Echibeckia, 105
Echinacea 'Cheyenne Spirit'
    Coneflower, 103
Echinacea purpurea
    Conefower, 102
Eupatorium
    Joe Pye Weed, 126
evergreens, 177
feeder roots, 156
foliar sprays, 176
Forthysia, 34
fungal attack, 176
Gaillardia
    Blanket Flower, 91
Galanthus
    Snowdrops, 22

Gaura, 137
Geranium 'Rozanne'
    Perennial Geranium, 88
glacial activity, 13
Hamamelis x intermedia
    Witch Hazel, 25
harden off, 155
hardiness zones, 12
healthy roots, 175
Helianthus
    Sunflower, 129
Hellebore 'Shooting Star', 21
Hellebores
    Lenten Rose, 21
Helleborus 'Champion', 31
Helleborus 'Dark and Handsome', 30
Helleborus 'Merlin', 24
Hemerocallis
    Daylily, 86
Heuchera
    Coral Bells, 92
hummingbirds, 61, 107, 126, 135, 152
Hyacinth, 32
Hydrangea 'Little Lime', 114
Hydrangea 'Tardiva', 121
Hydrangea macrophylla 'Bailmer'
    Endless Summer Hydrangea Mophead, 98
Hydrangea macrophylla 'Twist & Shout'
    Lacecap Hydrangea, 99
Ilex meserveae 'Golden Girl'

GARDENING BY MONTH

Gold Fruited Holly, 160
Ilex Nellie Stevens
    Nellie Stevens Holly, 169
Ilex verticillata
    Winterberry, 159
Ilex verticillata 'Afterglow'
    Winterberry, 161
Iris germanica
    Tall Bearded Iris, 58
Iris reticulata, 23
is 'Autumn Joy', 123
Itoh Peony 'Bartzella'
    Peony, 62
Japanese Andromeda 'Cavatine'
    Lilly of the Valley Shrub, 48
Japanese Anemone, 151
jelly, 167
Knock Out Rose, 72
Kousa Dogwood
    Japanese or Chinese Dogwood, 79
Lagerstroemia indica
    Crape Myrtle, 116
Lavender, 109
Leucanthemum
    Shasta Daisy, 89
Liatris spicata
    Blazing Star, 127
Ligularia
    Leopard Plant, 101
Lilium 'Casa Blanca', 111
Lilium 'Stargazer', 112
lime, 16
Liriope 'Variegata'
    Lillyturf, 132
Lobelia
    Cardinal Flower, 138

Lonicera sempervirens
    Trumpet Honeysuckle, 152
Lythrum virgatum, 106
Magnolia stellata 'Royal Star', 40
Mahonia
    Oregon Grape Holly, 166
Miscanthus 'Adiago', 133
Miscanthus sinensis 'Yaku Jima'
    Dwarf Maiden Grass, 133
Monarda
    Bee Balm, 100
Muscari, armenicum
    Grape Hyacinth, 43
Narcissus pseudonarcissus
    Daffodils, 33
Nepeta
    Catmint, 84
Nipponanthemum nipponicum
    Montauk Daisy, 146
organic fertilizer, 179
Over-seeding, 180
Paeonia 'Karl Rosenfeld', 63
Pelletized lime, 16
Pennisetum alopecuroides 'Hameln', 133
perennials, 178
Perovskia
    Russian Sage, 125
Phlox paniculata
    Tall Summer Phlox, 115
Platycodon
    Balloon Flower, 107
Powdery Mildew, 176
Prickly Pear Cactus, 94

Pruning, 155
Prunus 'Snofozam'
   Weeping Snow Fountain Cherry, 78
Prunus cerasifera 'Krauter Vesuvius'
   Flowering Plum, 41, 42
Prunus laurocerasus 'Otto Luyken'
   Cherry Laurel, 77
Prunus serrulata
   Kwanzan Cherry, 52
Prunus subhirtella
   Weeping Cherry, 78
Pulmonaria 'Majeste'
   Lungwort, 48
Rhododendron 'Roseum Elegans', 64
rose care, 178
Rudbeckia, 104
   Black Eyed Susan, 104
Salix caprea 'Pendula'
   Weeping Pussy Willow, 36
Salvia nemerosa
   Perennial Sage, 61
scale, 176
Sedum, 122, 123, 124
Sedum intermedia 'Lime Twister', 124
Sedum spectabile 'Autumn Joy', 123
Sedum spectabile 'Brilliant', 122
Shot Hole Fungus, 176
Siberian Iris, 57
Skip Laurel, 77
sod lawns, 179
Soil pH, 15
soil types, 14
Solidago sphacelata
   Autumn Goldenrod, 128
Spirea japonica 'Magic Carpet'
   Magic Carpet Spirea, 81
spring flowering bulbs, 142
St. Johnswort
   Hypercium, 136
stonecrop, 122
Syringa 'Penda' (Bloomerang Lilac, 65
Syringa patula 'Miss Kim', 66
   Korean Lilac, 66
Syringa vulgaris
   Common Lilac, 65
systemic applications, 176
Tricyrtis hirta
   Toad Lily, 150
Tulips, 45
Veronica,
   Speedwell, 85
Viburnum 'Summer Snowflake', 74
Viburnum dilatatum 'Cardinal Candy', 149
watering, 175
Weigela florida 'Spilled Wine', 75
Winter Aconite, 28
winter burn, 177
Wisteria floribunda, 76
Wisteria frutescens
   American Wisteria, 76

GARDENING BY MONTH

Made in United States
North Haven, CT
09 July 2022